CONTENTS

YOUR MONEY AND BENEFITS

BE SURE YOU COLLECT ALL THE BENEFITS YOU'RE ENTITLED TO

Source: **Judith A. Stein**, an attorney and executive director of the Center for Medicare Advocacy, Inc. She is president of the National Academy of Elder Law Attorneys.

Don't let ignorance or false pride prevent you from getting all you're entitled to in the way of aid when you retire. Some of the benefits may surprise you.

Some are provided on the basis of age alone...others depend on financial need.

AGE-BASED BENEFITS...

These benefits are yours simply because you've reached a certain birthday. **INCLUDED...**

• *Social Security benefits.* As a general rule, provided you've worked for a certain number of years over your lifetime, you qualify for Social Security benefits starting at age 62...though the benefits are reduced at that age.

Full benefit checks don't begin until your normal retirement age—currently age 65, but it will increase to 67 over the next several years.

Spouses, former spouses and widow(er)s may be entitled to benefits based on the other spouse's (or former spouse's) earnings and may start as early as age 60.

• *Medicare.* Unless you receive Social Security disability benefits for 24 months, your Medicare coverage doesn't start until age 65, even if you elected to begin receiving Social Security benefits at age 62.

Once you turn 65, you're covered under Part A of Medicare (hospital, skilled nursing facility, home health and hospice coverage) if you worked a certain length of time.

To receive Part B of Medicare (doctors' coverage, some home health and other outpatient services), you must pay a monthly premium.

LOCAL BENEFITS...

Check local papers for seniors' activities and the minimum age for participation. Also look for discounts and other help.

WHAT YOU'LL FIND...

• *Clubs, trips and programs for seniors.* Local governments generally help seniors' groups that meet for social and recreational purposes.

EXAMPLES: Daily recreational facilities...bus trips to a wide variety of places...field programs.

• *Senior discounts.* Retailers may offer discounts to seniors of a certain age. Many places provide senior ID cards to those as young as age 50 (for example, members of the American Association of Retired Persons) that can be used to cash in on discounts in the area.

• *Help with local transportation.* Cities and counties, in many places, run bus services for seniors.

BENEFITS BASED ON NEED...

A number of benefits for seniors can only be obtained if there is a financial need. The eligibility requirements may change from year to year. **INCLUDED...**

• *Supplemental Security Income (SSI)* provides income to seniors.

• *Food stamps.* Monthly allotments are available for the purchase of food items. The amount depends on household size and income. *Note:* The right to food stamps is not dependent on age.

• *Meal programs.* Home-bound seniors may be entitled to receive daily meal deliveries.

• *Medicare beneficiary programs* provide assistance with premiums, deductibles and copayments.

These Medicare programs are entitled QMB, SLMB, QI-1 and QI-2—depending on the benefits provided. They are limited to those age 65 or older with financial need.

• *Medicaid* pays for medical costs for those age 65 or older who have income and assets below a certain level (which varies by state). It also provides coverage for the blind and disabled, regardless of age.

• *Prescription aid.* In some states, low-income prescription drug programs help those age 65 or older who do not have Medicaid or other insurance to cover drug costs.

• *Property tax relief* lets senior home owners reduce their property tax bill. Rules differ in each locality, but may provide relief of up to 50% of the bill for those age 65 or older with income below a certain amount.

• *Rent subsidies.* As with property tax relief, some localities provide rent assistance for those in need.

• *Home energy assistance* for both renters and home owners gives cash (or makes payments to energy suppliers) in some localities if monthly income is below a threshold amount.

NO MINIMUM AGE: There may not be any minimum age for eligibility for the following...

• *Emergency assistance cash* for food, rent, moving, etc., for those with income below SSI limits.

TO FIND OUT ABOUT BENEFITS...

There's an elder network operating in every state that can provide information and assistance. You can tap into this network by contacting your local agency on aging or state department on aging.

NOTE: If you're investigating benefits for someone else, you can obtain general information without authorization. But if you need to discuss confidential information with a particular governmental agency, you may need authorization from the person you're helping.

• *Departments on Aging.* Every state has some administrative agency or subdivision for the elderly. It may go by a different name in your location—Office of Aging, Commission on Aging, Division of Senior Services, etc. Some state departments have regional offices. This is your first contact point. **THIS STATE OFFICE CAN PROVIDE...**

• Information about benefits and eligibility requirements.

• Referral services to agencies providing specific types of assistance.

• *Federal resources.* The Social Security Administration can provide information and help on Social Security benefits, Medicare and more. 800-772-1213 or *www.ssa.gov.*

• *The Health Care Financing Administration* (HCFA) also provides information and help with Medicare. 800-633-4227 or *www.medicare.gov.*

• *Access America for Seniors* Web site makes it easier to connect with various federal agencies. *www.seniors.gov.*

• *Administration on Aging* provides information for older Americans about opportunities and services. *www.aoa.dhhs.gov.*

• *Department of Veterans Affairs* provides information about VA programs for veterans and their families. 800-827-1000 or *www.va.gov.*

• *Private seniors organizations.* They can give you information on assistance programs. **THESE ORGANIZATIONS INCLUDE...**

• American Association of Retired Persons (AARP) at 800-424-3410 or *www.aarp.org.*

• Gray Panthers at 800-280-5362 or *www.graypanthers.org.*

• Older Women's League (OWL) at 800-825-3695 or *www.owl-national.org.*

• *The Center for Medicare Advocacy* provides assistance regarding Medicare and health-care rights. 860-456-7790 or *www.medicareadvocacy.org.*

• *Other organizations.* The National Academy of Elder Law Attorneys (NAELA) distributes brochures to explain various benefit programs for the elderly. 520-881-4005 or *www.naela.org.*

■

HOW TO LIVE BETTER, LESS EXPENSIVELY AND WITH STYLE

Source: **Ernest Callenbach**, a Berkeley, CA-based writer, lecturer and editor on ecological issues. He is author of *Living Cheaply with Style*. Ronin Publishing.

You don't need to spend a lot of money to have a quality lifestyle. In fact, by spending *less* you may *improve* your quality of life...

LIVE BETTER FOR LESS...

The quality of your life and health, your monetary expenditures and your contributions to the community are all interrelated. I call the connection of these three factors the "green triangle."

Surprisingly often, by taking steps to improve any *one* of these, you will improve the other two as well. **EXAMPLES...**

• *Reduce your consumption of high-fat meat* and improve your health, lower your food costs for these expensive foods and help the environment. Meat production is highly resource intensive: It is estimated that it takes about seven pounds of grain to produce one pound of meat.

• *Instead of driving your car for short trips, walk or bicycle.* You'll get healthful exercise, save expensive operating costs for your car and reduce the amount of pollution your car spews into the environment.

There are countless other cases where people can do well by themselves and others around them by spending less.

When retirement approaches: Reexamine health and money habits formed during working years. As health issues become more important and income becomes fixed, you may want to improve your health and money habits.

Awareness of the "green triangle" helps people change their habits by keeping in front of them the fact that they can obtain *multiple* benefits by doing so—saving money, improving quality of life and health and aiding the community. **MORE IDEAS...**

• *Eat at home more often.* You will slash your food costs with home-prepared meals. You will also improve your diet, since it is hard to avoid consuming too much fat and salt in restaurant meals. And by entertaining friends at home, you will improve your social life. Improving your cooking skills also can be a rewarding hobby for which you may have newfound time after retirement.

• *Eat out at lunch rather than dinner.* (Save half of what you order for a quick lunch or tomorrow's dinner.) You'll get the same quality food as you would for dinner but for a much lower price.

• *Own fewer objects—to simplify your life.* There's a natural tendency to believe that possessing "more things" will make us happy.

But the things we own also take energy and resources. Money must be spent buying and maintaining them. And care and effort must be expended tending them.

BEST: Take an inventory of all your possessions. Identify those that truly add value to your life and give you pleasure and those that don't. Then rid yourself of those that cost more in time, trouble or money to maintain than they are worth.

HOW: Sell them in a yard sale...auction them over the Internet at a site like eBay...donate them to charity...give them to family or friends.

Again, you will benefit in more than one way. As you simplify your life and reduce the demands placed on you as a result of owning so many things, you may also raise cash, get a tax deduction and secure the goodwill of family members and friends.

• *Keep a written record of every dollar you spend over a week or two.* Carry a pocket notebook with you and write down every expenditure you make.

BENEFIT: The record will give you a much better and surprising view of your money habits—and provide the concrete knowledge you need to improve them. It will also show you where you are spending money that is not adding to your quality of life—and where you are spending money that is.

By shifting your spending from the former items to the latter, you can improve the quality of your life at no extra expense—perhaps even while saving money.

• *Resolve to take charge of your health.* Doctors are not in charge of your health—you are. Realize this, become informed about the medical and health issues you face and take responsibility for tending to them every day.

By taking charge of your health, you reduce your need for doctors. You will also improve your physical quality of life and reduce the expenses you incur on treatment.

• *Make younger friends.* This can be important to your welfare as you get older. People naturally lose old friends as they age—some move to distant locations, others die.

But having friends is important not only for a satisfying lifestyle, but also for mental and physical health.

Having *younger* friends will keep you more engaged with new ideas and more physically active—and help you maintain a younger attitude and lifestyle for yourself.

New, younger friends will keep you from becoming isolated —and also from becoming a fuddy-duddy.

• *Buy a house.* During your later working years, it's a good idea to buy a home if you don't own one already.

WHY: In subsequent retirement years, you may become short of cash, but you will be *secure* if you own your own home.

Moreover, if need be, you can rent out part of your home to generate cash income. And if you become physically weakened by advancing age, you can even take in a caregiver and perhaps avoid having to move to a nursing home.

STASH YOUR CASH

Source: **Roger Klein, PhD,** president, Interest Rate Futures Research Corp., Mercerville, NJ.

Best place to park cash depends on your time horizon. *Best if you can tie up funds for at least six months:* Certificates of deposit. The highest rates usually come from out-of-town and Internet banks. *For current rates: www.bankrate.com. Best for total liquidity:* Federally insured money market account...or money market fund, which is not insured but is generally safe. *For best rates: www.imoneynet.com.*

VALUE OF OLD SAVINGS BONDS

Source: US Treasury Department, Bureau of the Public Debt, Washington, DC.

ables of Redemption Values for Savings Bonds, a free pamphlet from the US Treasury Department, tells what old bonds are worth and whether they still earn interest. Check their Web site at *www.publicdebt.treas.gov* or call 304-480-6112.

■

JUST IN CASE...

Source: **Terry Savage**, author, *The Savage Truth on Money* (John Wiley & Sons) and a syndicated *Chicago Sun–Times* financial columnist.

et up a home-equity line of credit *before* retiring or leaving a job in search of a new one. You may never need the money, but it's good to have the credit line available in an emergency. You may not be able to negotiate a credit line on the same terms when you are not working.

■

REDEEM E BONDS OR LOSE INTEREST

Source: **Barbara Weltman**, an attorney practicing in Millwood, NY, and author of *J.K. Lasser's Tax Deductions for Your Small Business, Fourth Edition* (John Wiley & Sons) and *The Complete Idiot's Guide to Making Money After You Retire* (Alpha Books).

ou may have been given US Series E or EE Savings Bonds as an anniversary gift or when you were married. Or maybe you even bought them through a payroll savings plan at work many years ago.

You probably stashed the bonds in the back of a drawer and then forgot about them, as so many people do.

PROBLEM: E and EE bonds stop paying interest when they reach their final maturity date. The Federal Reserve says there are now $6.2 billion worth of unredeemed savings bonds that are no longer paying interest.

WHAT TO DO: Dig out your savings bonds and turn them in if they've matured. Put the money in something that pays interest.

E bonds issued before December 1965 have a 40-year final maturity, so a bond issued in March 1960 stopped paying interest in March 2000.

E bonds issued from December 1965 through June 1980 and EE bonds issued from January 1980 onward have a final maturity of 30 years, so a bond issued in March 1970 stopped paying interest in March 2000.

DEFERRING TAXES: When you redeem the bonds, instead of paying tax on all the interest that has accrued, you can roll them over into US Government Series HH bonds.

HH bonds pay interest semiannually, but you will put off paying tax on your EE bonds until the HH bonds mature. HH bonds reach their final maturity after 20 years.

■

INVESTMENT STRATEGIES

THE BETTER WAY TO INVEST IN INDEX FUNDS

Source: **David Yeske, CFP,** president of the financial-planning and investment-management firm Yeske & Co., 220 Bush St., San Francisco 94104. He is a personal finance columnist for *San Francisco* magazine.

At a time when the number of critics of indexed investing is growing, there is one way to index that is gaining popularity. Here is how it works...

VERY, VERY EFFICIENT...

While you can buy indexed mutual funds, the most cost- and tax-efficient way to index today uses Exchange-Traded Funds (ETFs).

ETFs are like mutual funds, designed to mirror the performance of a market index, stock market sector or economic sector.

But rather than being purchased through a management company, ETFs trade on stock exchanges—generally the

American Stock Exchange (ASE)—as do common stocks. Any broker can execute a trade for an ETF.

The first ETF was the Standard & Poor's Depositary Receipt (SPDR or, more popularly, Spider), created in 1993 to track the S&P 500.

Today there are 70 ETFs with assets of $88 billion. The lineup now includes...

• *Spiders (SPDRs).* Now Spiders track the S&P Midcap index ...as well as such sectors as energy, financial services and technology.

• *Diamonds* track the Dow Jones Industrial Average.

• *Qubes* track the NASDAQ 100 Composite stocks. The name is a play on words, since the ticker symbol is QQQ.

• *Holdrs.* These Merrill Lynch ETFs track sectors such as pharmaceuticals and biotechnology and market indexes such as the Russell 2000.

• *iShares.* From Barclays Global Investors, iShares offer the largest number of ETFs, covering every major US and foreign stock market index.

• *StreetTracks,* from State Street Global Advisors, cover the Dow Jones and Morgan Stanley indexes.

MUTUAL FUNDS vs. ETFs...

• *Buying and selling.* Unlike regular mutual funds, for which purchases and sales are executed at the end of the trading day, ETFs trade throughout the day.

RESOURCES: To find price information on ETFs, go to the American Stock Exchange Web site, *www.amex.com,* and click on Index Shares or Holdrs.

A few mutual fund Web sites, *www.wiesenberger.com* and *www.morningstar.com* among them, offer performance information on ETFs.

• *Minimum initial investment.* $2,000 is the average. Many ETFs sell at less than $20 a share.

• *Sales and commissions.* You'll pay a brokerage commission to buy and sell ETF shares—less than $20 a trade with a discount broker. So index funds are better for small, steady investments. While no-load mutual funds carry no commission, funds that are sold by brokers carry front-end sales loads of about 5%.

• *Fees:* ETF expenses can be much less than those for regular index mutual funds. Both index funds and ETFs have far lower expenses than actively managed funds.

EXAMPLE: The iShares S&P 500 has annual expenses of 0.09%, while Vanguard's S&P 500 index fund charges 0.18%.

BONUS FOR AGGRESSIVE INVESTORS: Because ETFs trade as common stocks, you can sell them short (borrow the shares and sell them with the aim of repurchasing them at a lower price). But you can't do that with mutual funds.

TAXES MAKE THE BIG DIFFERENCE...

The biggest advantage of ETFs over mutual funds is the control you gain over tax planning.

• *Funds and taxes.* All capital gains realized by a mutual fund must be paid directly to shareholders. Your fund could have a net loss in a particular year. But if it sold investments at a profit during the year, you would still incur a capital gains tax liability. And the fund manager—not you—has control over when an investment is sold.

• *ETFs and taxes.* You incur a tax liability only when you sell ETF shares at a profit—an event that you control.

IMPORTANT: One selling point for index mutual funds is that they do little selling—hence, they pay out little in taxable capital gains.

But in the unlikely event that a fund is forced to liquidate holdings to meet a surge in redemptions, huge gains would be realized. There is no comparable risk with ETFs.

ADDED BENEFIT: Because ETFs don't face redemptions, they needn't hold a cash reserve, which is typically 4.5% for the average fund. ETFs can be fully invested in stocks...a prudent mutual fund can't.

ETF STRATEGY...

If you are investing in funds for a nonretirement account, you shouldn't sell your index funds to buy ETFs because of the tax consequences.

But consider putting new money in ETFs.

Here is how I would structure a diversified portfolio of ETFs...

• *US large-cap.* My benchmark would be the S&P 500. For an ETF, I would choose between the following...

- iShare S&P 500. ASE:IVV.
- Standard & Poor's Depositary Receipt. ASE:SPY.
- *US small-cap.* My benchmark would be the S&P Small-Cap 600. My ETF would be...
  - iShare S&P 600. ASE:IJR.
- *Domestic value.* I like to include a value component in any portfolio. While you could buy ETF sector funds in each of the most depressed sectors, buying an entire value index diversifies your bet. Choose between the following...
  - iShare Russell 1000 Value. ASE:IWD.
  - iShare S&P 500 Value. ASE: IVE.
- *Domestic growth.* Choose between the following...
  - iShare Russell 1000 Growth. ASE:IWF.
  - iShare S&P 500 Growth. ASE:IVW.
- *Investing abroad.* Every portfolio needs foreign exposure. Six ETFs cover 70% to 80% of the world. Here are my suggested foreign-market ETFs and percentages of foreign allocation...
  - 25%/iShares MSCI Japan. ASE:EWJ.
  - 22%/iShares MSCI United Kingdom. ASE:EWU.
  - 15%/iShares MSCI Germany. ASE:EWG.
  - 15%/iShares MSCI France. ASE:EWQ.
  - 10%/iShares MSCI Australia. ASE:EWA.
  - 8%/iShares MSCI Switzerland. ASE:EWL.
  - 5%/iShares MSCI Netherlands. ASE:EWN.

■

PORTFOLIO READJUSTMENT STRATEGY

Source: **Lewis J. Altfest, CFP,** president, L.J. Altfest & Co., Inc., a fee-only financial planning firm, 116 John St., New York 10038. He is professor of finance at Pace University in New York.

The Federal Reserve seems to have done a good job of balancing the economy, getting rid of the overexuberance of the stock market and yet keeping us out of recession—the essentially soft landing that economists have been predicting. I'm advising my older clients to be conservative, though.

In terms of overall allocation, I am recommending that they have no more than 65% in stocks—with 35% in bonds.

THE SHIFT TO VALUE...

The recent correction in the overvalued technology and telecommunications sectors caused major disappointments for many shareholders.

Now is a good time to look at your portfolio from a fundamental point of view. Forget "sex appeal" and take price into account. Consider shifting from tech stocks to value stocks. This shift is already beginning to happen in the marketplace, where we're seeing a resurgence of the so-called "old economy" stocks of the Dow and the S&P 500. Actually, the old and new economies are coming together as all companies adapt to new technology. There's only one economy, after all.

Of course, you want to own some growth companies, but for now, I advise clients to allocate more to value, aiming to have up to half of their stock portfolios in value-oriented stocks and mutual funds.

GUIDELINE: The 50-20 rule. Don't buy—and/or lighten up on—anything that has a price/earnings (P/E) multiple of more than 50.

Instead, favor stocks selling for less than a 20 P/E multiple, the lower the better, so long as the company has solid fundamentals in sales and earnings growth...and strong management.

I anticipate a continuing peaceful transition from stocks with high P/Es to those with low P/Es, without the market collapsing. I don't see a recession near-term. The Fed has the economy in control.

MUTUAL FUND SELECTIONS...

The value-oriented no-load mutual funds that I like now are...

• *Vanguard Windsor II* (VWNFX). 800-523-1154. A large-cap fund.

• *Royce Opportunity* (RYPNX). 800-221-4268. An investment-class fund that concentrates on small- and micro-cap companies with capitalizations under $1.5 billion.

For some international representation (about 20%), which all investors should have today, I like...

• *Tweedy Browne Global Value Fund* (TBGVX). 800-432-4789. Looks for undervalued stocks throughout the world, including the US.

BOND FUND SELECTIONS...

Now bonds are looking better than many stocks. Top-rated corporates (AA, A) are yielding relatively more than Treasuries than they have for a long time. But you need a good professional bond-fund manager to get the most benefit from this situation. My favorite now...

• *Loomis Sayles Bond Fund* (LSBRX). 800-633-3330.

I don't even mind junk bonds right now because they are selling at a discount due to fears of economic slowdown or recession. Just be sure to avoid funds that have a large portion in low-rated communications industry bonds. A conservative selection in the high-yield sector...

• *Vanguard High Yield Corporate Fund* (VWEHX). 800-523-1154. Invests in a diversified portfolio of junk bonds, with 80% rated B or higher. Also, it can hedge up to 20% of its assets.

∎

WHAT TOP PLANNERS ARE TELLING CLIENTS

Sources: **Lewis J. Altfest, CFP**, president, L.J. Altfest & Co., Inc., a fee-only financial planning firm, 116 John St., New York 10038...**Harold Evensky, CFP**, principal, Evensky, Brown & Katz, 241 Sevilla Ave., Suite 902, Coral Gables, FL 33134...and **Laurence I. Foster, CPA/PFS**, Richard A. Eisner & Company, LLP, 575 Madison Ave., New York 10022.

Most investors age 50 and older are especially concerned about protecting their nest eggs.

Here's what three of the country's top financial planners are advising clients now...

LEWIS J. ALTFEST
L. J. ALTFEST & CO., INC.

Review your stock holdings—to be sure that the companies you're holding have earnings.

Few people over age 50 should be primarily invested in Internet stocks. Internet investments are OK for play money, but you have to be more serious about your money as you approach retirement. You want companies with reasonable valuations and favorable earnings outlooks.

Avoid anything provocative, that is, anything with a price/ earnings ratio over 50.

TIPS: Given the current outlook, I like *TIPS*—Treasury Inflation-Protected Securities. They provide conservative investors with guaranteed real returns (after adjusting for inflation) if held to maturity. They are available in different amounts and maturities.

Currently, you can earn a 7% return, but more important, a real total return of 4.11% on a 10-year TIPS note *with little risk.*

You can buy TIPS through a broker or direct from the Treasury.

ASSET ALLOCATION: I favor 60% stocks and 40% bonds for conservative investors. I would underweight technology in the portfolio and overweight value stocks—rather than growth stocks. You might break down the 60% in stocks as follows, with my favorite no-load funds...

20% IN A LARGE-CAP VALUE FUND...

• *Vanguard Windsor II* (VWNFX). 800-523-7731.

9% IN A MEDIUM-CAP FUND...

• *Longleaf Partners Fund* (LLPFX). 800-445-9469.

9% IN A SMALL-CAP FUND...

• *Royce Opportunity Fund* (RYPNX). 800-221-4268.

7% IN REIT FUNDS...

• *Cohen & Steers Realty Shares* (CSRSX). 800-330-7348.

• *Fidelity Real Estate Investment Portfolio* (FRESX). 800-544-8888.

REITs have a high yield and have the potential for capital gains as well. They're also a hedge against the stock market.

15% IN AN INTERNATIONAL FUND...

• *Tweedy, Browne Global Value Fund* (TBGVX). 800-432-4789.

HAROLD EVENSKY
EVENSKY, BROWN & KATZ

My advice to conservative investors is to focus on high quality, be tax conscious and be well diversified.

• *Ladder your holdings* so that maturities are spread over a number of years.

• *Never try to time the market.* You won't win.

• *Hold bonds as well as stocks.* The asset allocation that has been the most efficient, historically, is 60% stocks, 40% bonds. That's a sensible starting point for investors now.

KEY: Make sure you have enough cash and short-term securities to meet your needs for two years.

Then, I'd break down the 60% stocks into 45% domestic and 15% international. Of domestic stocks, I'd put 30% to 35% in large-cap equities...and 10% to 15% in small- and mid-caps. Here are my favorite funds now in the various categories...

Domestic large-cap funds...

• *Schwab 1000 Fund* (SNXFX). 800-435-4000.

• *Vanguard 500 Index* (VFINX). 800-523-7731.

• *Wilshire Target Large Company Growth* (DTLGX). 888-200-6796.

• *Wilshire Target Large Company Value* (DTLVX). 888-200-6796.

SMALL- AND MID-CAP FUNDS...

• *Accessor Small to Mid Cap Portfolio* (ACMCX). 800-759-3504.

• *Undiscovered Managers Behavioral Growth Fund* (UBRLX). 888-242-3514.

INTERNATIONAL FUNDS...

• *Matthews Pacific Tiger Fund* (MAPTX). 800-789-2742.

• *Montgomery International Growth Fund* (MNIGX). 800-572-3863.

• *SSgA Emerging Markets Fund* (SSEMX). 800-647-7327.

For the bond portion, select funds from the wide spectrum of taxable or tax-exempt choices from these three fund families...

• *Federated Funds.* 800-245-4270.

• *PIMCO.* 888-877-4626.

• *Vanguard Funds.* 800-523-7731.

LAURENCE I. FOSTER
RICHARD A. EISNER & COMPANY, LLP

Investment allocation is a very individual matter. I don't believe that there are any simple answers.

No matter what the market is doing right now, I start by looking at what a client already has and comparing that with what he/she needs in the way of income. We ask clients to recap all expenditures for the past several years, beginning with rough estimates that can be developed in detail later.

Next, we look at current sources of income. The client may still be earning an income. And—there may be a pension, Social Security, bank accounts and a current portfolio of assets, including 401(k) and other retirement income, too. *Note:* To avoid a 10% penalty on pension payouts, you generally must be over age 59½.

KEY: What is the total of all usable income? If that falls short of your needs, single out investments that are not producing income.

Many technology stocks produce no current income and may not for years to come. Consider replacing them with moderate-risk blue-chip stocks that pay a dividend and also offer potential growth to offset inflation.

Examine pension and retirement accounts to see how they're invested.

EXAMPLE: If a pension fund is heavily invested in bonds, you can feel comfortable putting more of your own retirement account in stocks, even growth stocks.

People who are depending on their investment portfolio for every penny of income may want to stay 100% in fixed-income securities. In a rising interest rate environment, bonds (whose prices usually go down as interest rates rise) are risky to buy—especially if you are apt to need the money before maturity.

If, say, you are contemplating a substantial move in a few years, you will need available cash. Don't tie it up in the volatile stock market, in fixed-income securities or where you could lose capital.

In the final analysis, some clients may find that they must alter their lifestyle and reduce expenditures to accommodate income realities.

Or the lucky ones may develop new sources of income, such as payback contributions from their children. So, everyone's solution is different. It depends on the facts and circumstances.

■

GREAT TAX BREAKS FOR HOME OWNERS

Source: **Laurence I. Foster, CPA/PFS,** partner, personal financial planning practice, Richard A. Eisner & Company, LLP, 575 Madison Ave., New York 10022. Mr. Foster is former chairman, estate planning committee, New York State Society of Certified Public Accountants.

When young people seek to buy their first home, they often receive help from family.

But the IRS can help too—by providing tax breaks both for the home purchase itself and for family members who assist the home buyers financially...

HELP FROM PARENTS...

How parents and others can help young home buyers...

• *Tax-free gifts.* Parents or others can make tax-free gifts to a home buyer to help cover the cost of the down payment on a home.

Every individual can make gifts of up to $10,000 per recipient per year that are exempt from gift tax. So a home buyer could receive several $10,000 gifts from different family members. Married couples can jointly make tax-free gifts of up to $20,000 ($40,000 if joint gifts are made to a child and a child's spouse).

Even larger gifts can be made without incurring current gift tax by using part of your lifetime gift and estate tax credit ($675,000 in 2001).

ADVANTAGE: Such a gift may reduce future estate taxes by reducing the size of the gift maker's estate—especially if the gift funds were invested in appreciating assets.

SPECIAL HELP: If you are going to help a home purchaser with a gift, make a gift large enough to enable the buyer to avoid having to pay for mortgage insurance. Generally, such insurance is required when the down payment covers less than 20% of the home's value.

Avoiding the cost of the insurance premiums eliminates a charge against family wealth.

• *Interest-free loans.* In some cases, it may be better to help a home buyer with an interest-free loan rather than a gift (assuming that this doesn't prevent the buyer from obtaining a mortgage). This can provide protection against unforeseen circumstances. **EXAMPLES...**

• Divorce. After making a gift to your child and his/her spouse to help them buy a home, they divorce—and the house goes to the spouse who's not your child. In that case, you'll never get your gift back.

However, if you made a loan to the couple that was secured by the home, the spouse who received the home would have to repay you.

• Hostile creditors. A home buyer may fall into trouble with creditors who threaten to seize the home. If you assisted with the purchase of the home through a gift, that money may be lost. But if you assisted with a loan that is secured by the home, you will get your money back—because you will be the first creditor in line to be repaid, usually after the first mortgage.

Retain the option of being repaid in the future—perhaps when the home buyer is better established financially and you have greater need of the money.

If all goes well between both the home buyer and yourself, you can later forgive up to $10,000 of the loan annually as a tax-free gift (or up to $20,000 as a joint gift).

• *Co-ownership.* When a person can't qualify to buy a home alone, a parent or other family member may buy the house with the child as a co-owner.

The parent can then charge the child rent and claim the tax benefits of owning a rental property.

Depreciation and other rental expenses may shelter rental income from tax, turning the home into a tax shelter for the co-owner. And if the home appreciates in value, it may be an attractive investment as well.

For the co-owner to deduct tax losses, a fair rental must be charged to the child for the partial interest in the house that is rented. But a fair rent need not be full market rent—the Tax Court has stated that a discount of as much as 20% below market rent may be fair when renting to a family member because of the reduced risk involved. [Bindseil, TC Memo 1983-411.]

Investment rules rather than residential tax rules apply to the outside co-owner of the home. For instance, the tax exclusion for up to $500,000 of gain on a home sale won't be available to the nonresident buyer. So consult an expert before acting.

ADDITIONAL TAX BREAKS...

• *IRA withdrawals.* Up to $10,000 total during the taxpayer's lifetime can be withdrawn from an IRA before age 59½ without penalty when used toward the cost of a first-time home buyer's purchase of a home.

First-time home buyer is defined as a person who has not owned a principal residence within the prior two years. A withdrawal can be made to help a spouse, child, grandchild, or parent or grandparent buy a home.

While the IRA withdrawal escapes penalty, it is still subject to income tax under normal rules.

And there's an extra cost as well—future tax deferrals are lost on the withdrawn funds. Money that is taken out of an IRA can't be replaced, and withdrawing $10,000 effectively costs five years of maximum contributions. So consider the total cost of this option before acting.

• *Loan origination fees or "points" incurred to buy a principal residence are fully deductible* (provided they are reasonable in amount in relation to normal local banking practices).

SNAG: Young home buyers with few deductible items other than mortgage interest may find it does not pay to itemize deductions. That's especially important if they buy a home late in the year, so the mortgage interest deduction for the year is small. In that case, they may not be able to deduct the points currently.

HELPFUL: The IRS has ruled that in such a case, a home buyer can elect to amortize the points over the life of the loan—spreading the deduction over later years, when it will be more valuable. [Letter Ruling 199905033.]

Points also are deductible when incurred on a loan used to improve a primary residence.

Points incurred on a refinancing must be amortized—but upon a subsequent refinancing, any points that remain undeducted from a previous refinancing become deductible.

• *Home-office deduction.* This deduction can offset normal home ownership costs—effectively providing a tax subsidy to a buyer who will qualify to claim it.

Normally nondeductible costs such as insurance and maintenance become deductible to the extent that they relate to the office. And depreciation is a no-cash-cost deduction that provides tax shelter benefits.

TO QUALIFY FOR THE DEDUCTION: A portion of the home must be used exclusively for business. The office also must be the principal place where a business is conducted...or be used to meet with customers or clients on a regular basis...or be necessary to maintain required records for a business primarily conducted elsewhere.

The part of the home that's used as an office for more than three of the five years before a sale will be treated as business property and will not qualify for the tax exclusion.

■

SOME WAYS TO INVEST IN A NEW BUSINESS ARE MUCH BETTER THAN OTHERS

Source: **Janice M. Johnson, JD, CPA,** managing director, financial services, American Express Tax and Business Services, Inc., 1185 Avenue of the Americas, New York 10036.

With the booming economy, more and more people are starting new businesses, and you may be offered the opportunity to invest in one. Or you may even be considering starting your own.

KEY: Start-up businesses offer the opportunity of big gains, but also always carry the risk of losses.

STRATEGY: Plan your investment to minimize taxes should it be profitable, and to maximize your deductions should a loss occur.

PLAN AHEAD...

Start by thinking ahead to your likely future situation, and consider how you will want to realize future gains or losses. If you are investing in a family business—such as by supporting a child's start-up business—consider estate planning as well as income taxes.

EXAMPLE: If you buy stock in a child's business that proves successful, you may increase your taxable estate.

Next, consider these investment options and strategies. Examine the consequences of each whether the investment makes or loses money. Then select the ideas that are best for you. **INVESTMENT STRATEGIES...**

- *Buy Section 1244 stock.* Normally a loss on a stock investment is a capital loss that is used to offset capital gain, with no more than $3,000 deductible against ordinary income per year.

But a loss on Section 1244 stock is fully deductible against ordinary income in an amount up to $100,000 on a joint return or $50,000 on a single return.

PAYOFF: Section 1244 provides the best of both worlds tax-wise—tax-favored capital gain if the stock goes up in value, and a fully deductible loss if its value declines.

Qualification requirements for Section 1244 stock...

- Stock must be issued by the company in exchange for cash or property—not bought from another shareholder.

- All the company's owners combined must not have contributed more than $1 million for their stock.

- The company cannot receive more than 50% of its gross receipts from royalties, rents, dividends, interest, annuities, and sales or exchanges of securities.

If qualification conditions are met, stock automatically becomes Section 1244 stock—no election need be filed.

- *Buy preferred stock.* This carries a fixed dividend that is paid before any dividend payment is made on common stock.

RESULT: The stock pays a stream of income that makes its value more stable than that of common stock, neither rising nor falling as much as that of common stock due to market conditions.

Consider preferred stock when...

- The business is profitable and you primarily wish to receive income from it, with some opportunity for appreciation in stock value.

- You invest in a family business and want most of the appreciation in its value to pass to younger owners who own its common stock.

- *Loan money to the business.* Instead of buying stock, loan funds to the business. This may be the simplest way to help someone start a business. ADVANTAGES...

- The person who starts the business retains full ownership and control of it.

- You receive a stream of income from the business through the loan repayments. These are paid before preferred stock dividends and are thus more secure than such dividends.

- The business can deduct its interest payments.
- You avoid stock appreciation in your taxable estate.

Drawbacks...

- The business incurs the cash drain of the loan repayments.

- No matter how profitable the business proves to be, you'll receive no more than the interest on the loan.

- If the business fails, the loss on the loan probably will be a capital loss—deductible only against capital gain with no more than $3,000 deductible against ordinary income. (A loss suffered on a loan to a business is deductible as a business loss only if you are in the business of making such loans.)

IMPORTANT: Fully document any loan—especially one to a family member's business. Otherwise, the IRS may consider it a gift and allow no deduction for a loss on the loan at all.

TACTIC: Help a family member start a business with an interest-free loan. Such loans of up to $10,000 can be made with no adverse tax effect. Large loans may be advantageous too, but are subject to complex rules, so consult an expert.

ADVANTAGE: The family member receives funds to start a business without incurring interest charges. If the business fails, you retain the capital loss deduction for the loan. If it succeeds, you can forgive the loan through one or more tax-free gifts.

You effectively make a gift to help a family member start a business while retaining some "deduction protection" for yourself should the business fail.

You can make tax-free gifts of up to $10,000 each to as many different recipients as you wish annually—and the limit is $20,000 when gifts are made jointly with a spouse.

- *Lease property to the business.* Instead of contributing property (such as real estate or equipment) to a business for stock or providing cash to the business that it will use to buy such property, consider personally owning the property and leasing it to the business. **ADVANTAGES...**

- If the business fails, the property will not be lost.

- Depreciation deductions on the property can offset the lease payments, creating a tax-sheltered stream of income. And the same payments are deductible by the business.

- The property avoids being locked into the business. You retain much more flexibility to dispose of or finance the property as you wish.

FORM OF BUSINESS...

In addition to the type of investment you make, also consider the form of business you wish to invest in. It can make a big difference tax-wise.

If you are there at the beginning, select the form of business that is best for you.

• *S corporation.* Gains and losses of an S corporation are reported on the tax returns of their shareholders in proportion to their holdings. **RESULT...**

• If the business loses money, perhaps during the start-up stage, investors can deduct the losses on their personal tax returns.

• If the business makes money, owners report the income on their personal returns.

STRATEGY: Invest in a new S corporation as a shareholder and deduct its start-up losses on your personal tax return at your top tax-bracket rate. After the business becomes profitable, make gifts of your shares to younger family members to remove them from your taxable estate and move the income on them into lower tax brackets.

NOTE: The stock of an S corporation can qualify as Section 1244 stock.

• *Limited Liability Company (LLC) or Limited Liability Partnership (LLP).* These are entities that, like corporations, provide their owners with protection against personal liability for the business's debts.

LLCs and LLPs are taxed on a pass-through basis much like S corporations, but often with more flexibility. **ADVANTAGES...**

• As partnerships, their gains and losses can be distributed to owners disproportionately to ownership holdings, creating more opportunities for income shifting and deduction shifting.

• They avoid many complications that corporations incur— such as the double taxation of income first to a corporation and then to its owners.

DRAWBACKS: Investors in LLCs and LLPs who participate in any way in a business may be subject to employment tax on all their income from it. This is a gray area of the law.

It is much easier for an S corporation to minimize employment taxes by giving its owner/executive the minimum reasonable salary. All other distributions on shares escape employment tax.

■

BIOTECH INVESTING

Source: **James E. Moltz**, vice chairman and chief equity strategist, International Strategy & Investment Group, 535 Madison Ave., New York 10022.

Despite the danger of Washington meddling in drug pricing, pharmaceuticals and medical services will be a good place to be invested in the next several years.

FAVORABLE FACTORS: An aging population and exciting biotech advances that could result in mergers between biotech companies and big pharmaceuticals.

HIS PICKS: Johnson & Johnson, Merck and Pfizer among traditional drug stocks...Amgen in the biotech area...and Medtronic in medical devices.

■

GO TO THE SOURCE

Source: **Matthew Sitler**, director, shareholder services, Georgeson Shareholder Communications Inc., 17 State St., 28th fl., New York 10004.

Direct Purchase Plans (DPPs) let small investors buy stock directly from companies—in some cases, even if you start with as little as $10. About 600 companies now have DPPs, including such well-known firms as Allstate, Campbell Soup, ExxonMobil and Wal-Mart. But the SEC does not let companies advertise DPPs aggressively, and brokers do not tell customers about them—since the plans let you buy without paying commissions.

MORE INFORMATION: Direct Purchase Plan Clearinghouse, 800-774-4117 or *www.enrolldirect.com.*

■

CHOOSE FUNDS WISELY

Source: **Sheldon Jacobs,** editor of *The No-Load Fund Investor,* 410 Saw Mill River Rd., Ardsley, NY 10502...**Don Phillips,** managing director of Morningstar, Inc., 225 W. Wacker Dr., Chicago 60606.

Don't rely on star ratings to choose funds. Morningstar rankings simply look at *past* performance. The risk-adjusted ratings change monthly, says a study in *Journal of Financial Planning*...and are awarded on a bell curve—so the top 10% of funds get five stars. Ratings were never intended to predict performance. *Better:* Look at investment style, peer comparisons and holdings in order to choose funds.

■

RETIREMENT
PLANNING

BULLETPROOF YOUR 401(K)
AGAINST A DECLINING MARKET

Source: **Martin D. Weiss**, editor of *Safe Money Report*, 4176 Burns Rd., Palm Beach Gardens, FL 33410.

There is more than $5 trillion invested in retirement plans today—most of it in equity funds. So many Americans have 401(k) plans that more than 40 million people would be at risk in a serious stock market decline. **WHAT TO DO IF YOU'RE NERVOUS...**

• *Don't pull money out.* Even if the investment options are limited, most plans offer alternatives that are safer than the stock market. (Under the law, retirement plans must offer at least three choices.)

• *Choose safety over yield.*

• *Come as close to a Treasury-only money market mutual fund as possible.* If your plan does not offer a pure Treasury-only money market fund, choose the safest alternative—a government-only money market fund. Barring that, pick any money market fund. They've had a strong record of safety. Next, a bond fund is almost always safer than a stock fund.

• *Fight.* If your 401(k) plan doesn't offer nonstock alternatives, get together with colleagues and petition your employer for more choices.

■

HOW TO HAVE A STEADY INCOME FOR LIFE

Source: **Robert M. Freedman, Esq.**, Freedman and Fish, 260 Madison Ave., New York 10016. Mr. Freedman is former chairman of the elder law section of the New York State Bar Association and founder of the National Academy of Elder Law Attorneys.

The peace of mind that comes from knowing you'll have a steady income for life comes at a price—your assets will decline rather than grow. But if lifetime income is your goal, there are a number of ways to achieve it...

RETIREMENT PLANS...

When you retire, you'll likely have a choice of how to take your money from the company pension plan. Many financial advisers suggest rolling over a company retirement plan distribution into an IRA to retain maximum flexibility. When the money is in an IRA, you can invest it as you see fit. And you'll have full access to the funds at all times. But if a steady income for life is your primary goal, you may want to have the pension money paid to you in monthly installments. If your spouse survives you, he/she can continue to receive a monthly income for life.

CAUTION: Once you've made the election to take pension distributions in the form of a monthly annuity, you can't change your mind.

ALTERNATIVE: Roll over pension funds to an IRA, and, in effect, create your own fixed flow of income. Simply withdraw the IRA money in regular monthly installments.

SELF-DEFENSE: Sit down with a financial planner who can work out a withdrawal schedule to provide for a monthly income from the IRA (based on your life expectancy).

While distributions from your IRA must begin by April 1 of the year following the year you turn 70½—you can *start* taking your annuity payments from the IRA at any younger age you choose. (If you're under age 59½, though, you'll be assessed a 10% early withdrawal penalty, unless payments are made in a series of substantially equal periodic payments.)

BUY A COMMERCIAL ANNUITY...

Those who lack the experience of handling large sums of money may want to use insurance proceeds or other lump-sum payments to buy lifetime income from an insurance company in the form of an annuity.

Commercial annuities are investment products offered by insurance companies. They are bought directly from the company or through banks and brokerage firms. The insurance company paying on the life insurance policy can provide an annuity, but shop around to find the best one for you.

From an investment perspective, commercial annuities may not appeal to you. You must consider the fees the company charges for the annuity in relation to the return.

But if you're prepared to pay the price and the insurance company is sound, then peace of mind can be yours with a commercial annuity.

INCOME OPTION...

Annuities pay a fixed monthly amount to you during your lifetime and can be tailored to provide a continued flow of income to your surviving spouse.

TURNING ASSETS INTO INCOME...

• *Reverse mortgages.* Older people of moderate means can convert the equity in their home into a monthly retirement income by using a reverse mortgage. Instead of paying principal and interest monthly, you receive a monthly check.

General qualifications...

• Generally you must be age 62 or older.

• There must be little or no other mortgage on the home.

• The home must be single family (or a one-unit condominium that is FHA-approved) and owner-occupied. Owners of mobile homes don't qualify for reverse mortgages.

The monthly income you receive is fixed according to the value of your home, the area in which you live (FHA-insured reverse mortgages set maximum loan caps for various areas) and your current age. There are different payment options to choose from, one being a monthly income for life (or the joint life of the home owners).

CAUTION: The reverse mortgage becomes due when the owner sells the home, moves or dies.

CHARITABLE REMAINDER TRUSTS...

If you have substantial assets, especially appreciated assets such as securities, you can use them to obtain a fixed income for life *and* benefit charity by setting up a charitable remainder trust. **BENEFITS...**

• *Fixed income.* You receive a fixed monthly income based on the value of the assets in the trust—and the type of charitable remainder trust you use.

You can even obtain inflation protection by using a charitable unitrust. It pays a monthly income based on a percentage of the value of the assets annually. If the assets' value rises, you benefit accordingly.

• *Tax deduction.* You can claim a current income tax deduction for the value of the "remainder interest" of the money that the charity will receive when you die. This deduction is determined by IRS tables.

CAUTION: To achieve tax benefits, the trust must be set up carefully. Consult an attorney for this purpose.

OTHER CHARITABLE OPTIONS...

Instead of using a personal charitable trust, consider...

• *Pooled income funds.* Your contribution to the charity goes into a pool with gifts from other donors. The money is invested by professional money managers.

Your income is based on the size of your gift and your age. You also receive an upfront tax deduction for the gift based on the value of what the charity will get upon your death.

• *Charitable gift annuity.* Some of the country's biggest charities will provide you with a monthly income and a tax deduction —in return for a hefty donation. The monthly income payments may not be as large as those from a commercial annuity, but you're providing a benefit to society rather than to an insurance company's shareholders.

■

SOCIAL SECURITY TAX-SAVING STRATEGY

Source: **Barbara Weltman**, an attorney practicing in Millwood, NY. She is author of *The Complete Idiot's Guide to Making Money After You Retire*. Alpha Books.

Social Security recipients lose a significant portion of benefits to taxes if their income exceeds certain limits. More specifically, when Modified Adjusted Gross Income (MAGI)—which is Adjusted Gross Income increased by tax-free interest on municipal bonds, certain exclusions and a portion of Social Security benefits—exceeds...

• *$32,000 on a joint return* or $25,000 on a single return, up to 50% of Social Security benefits are included in taxable income.

• *$44,000 on a joint return,* $34,000 on a single return or zero if married filing separately, up to 85% of Social Security benefits are included in taxable income.

TAX-SAVING STRATEGY: Reduce tax on your Social Security benefits by reducing your MAGI. **HOW...**

• *Defer Income.* Invest for growth rather than income. Postpone realizing gains on investments and taking discretionary distributions from IRAs and other retirement plans.

• *Make tax-free investments.* Roth IRA payouts of earnings are tax free if certain conditions are met, so fund a Roth IRA rather than a regular IRA.

Interest from tax-free municipal bonds is included in MAGI for purposes of determining tax on Social Security benefits—but municipals pay a lower interest rate than taxable bonds.

• *Shift income.* Make estate-tax-reducing gifts of property to younger family members by shifting income-producing property.

• *Deduct losses.* At year-end, take "paper" investment losses to offset income from gains and up to $3,000 of ordinary income. You can repurchase the loss investment after 31 days, or a similar but not identical one immediately.

■

EARLY RETIREMENT AND SOCIAL SECURITY BENEFITS

Source: **Peter J. Strauss, Esq.**, a partner in the law firm Epstein Becker & Green, PC, 250 Park Ave., New York 10017. He is a fellow of the National Academy of Elder Law Attorneys and coauthor of *The Elder Law Handbook—A Legal and Financial Survival Guide for Caregivers and Seniors.* Facts on File.

The age at which you can begin to collect full Social Security retirement benefits is going up. It will rise gradually, in two-month increments, from age 65 for persons born in 1938 and later, to age 67 in the year 2027.

ULTIMATE IMPACT: Persons born in 1960 and later won't be able to collect full benefits until they reach age 67.

The *early retirement age*, however, will not change. You'll still be able to begin collecting reduced Social Security benefits at age 62.

REDUCED BENEFITS...

If you were born in 1939, you will turn 62 in 2001. *Quandary:* When you opt for early retirement, your monthly benefits are reduced from what you'd get if you waited until the normal retirement age to start collecting Social Security.

The normal retirement age for a person born in 1939 is age 65 and four months. The benefit reduction for taking early retirement at 62 is 20% of what you'd get if you waited until age 65. Those who retire early must take a percentage reduction for each month that they retire before their "normal" retirement age. A percentage of the full benefit is lopped off.

The percentage of full benefits lost is five-ninths of 1% for the first 36 months of retirement before normal retirement age and five-twelfths of 1% for each additional month.

EXAMPLE I: A person born before 1938 who opts for early retirement at age 62 would have his/her monthly Social Security benefit check permanently reduced by 20% of the full retirement benefit. So, if benefits at 65 would be $1,000 a month, taking retirement at 62 will reduce benefits to $800 a month.

EXAMPLE II: Someone born after 1959 who takes early retirement at age 62 (when the normal retirement age has gone up to 67) will have benefits reduced by 30%. If full benefits are $1,000 a month, early retirement benefits will be $700 a month.

If you're thinking about early retirement, you need to get an estimate of your benefits. This is sent to you automatically about three months before your birthday if you are 25 years old or older. If you don't receive it, request it from the Social Security Administration at 800-SSA-1213 or from their Web site at *www.ssa.gov*.

SHOULD I TAKE EARLY RETIREMENT?

Opting for early retirement means that benefits commence early, before age 65, even though at a reduced rate.

ADVANTAGE: This gives you additional years of collecting benefits.

BOTTOM LINE: Suppose your normal retirement age is 65, but you take early retirement at 62 with reduced benefits. In terms of total benefits, you'll be ahead of what you would have received had you waited until age 65 to start collecting, until you reach a "crossover point" at age 77. Beyond that point your total benefits would be greater if you retired at age 65.

As the normal retirement age increases to age 67 (and the reduction in early retirement benefits also increases), it will take about 14 years (until the same age of 77) before the later retiree can catch up with the early retiree in total benefits received.

WORKING WHILE COLLECTING...

• *Under current law, retirement benefits are reduced for those under age 65* if their earnings from employment exceed a set amount. Then, Social Security benefits are reduced by $1 for each $2 of excess earnings.

• *Those between age 65 and age 70 can earn a greater amount* ($25,000 in 2001...$30,000 in 2002 and later years). Benefits are reduced by $1 for each $3 of excess earnings.

A bill to repeal the earnings limit for this age group was recently enacted by the Congress.

• *Those age 70 and older and still working are not subject to an earnings penalty* and can earn any amount without a reduction in benefits.

NOTE: The earnings limit does not change even though the normal retirement age has been increased.

If you plan to work full time or otherwise earn more than the modest earnings limit for those under age 65, it may not make sense to commence benefits before retirement.

MEDICARE...

Benefits under Medicare do not start before age 65. This is so even if you opt for early retirement at age 62.

However, the Medicare starting age does not change. This is the case even though the Social Security normal retirement age will increase. The Medicare eligibility age remains 65.

DECISIONS, DECISIONS...

Whether or not to start receiving Social Security benefits at the early retirement age depends on your personal situation. Questions to ask yourself...

• *Life expectancy.* What is your personal health history (and family health history)? If you do not anticipate a long life, then opting for early commencement of benefits may prove more financially rewarding than waiting until your normal retirement age.

• *Capacity for work.* If you are planning to continue at a job or to work at your own business, then waiting until you cease working—or, depending on your earnings, at least attain age 65—may make much more sense for you than starting benefits early.

■

KEY DECISIONS TO MAKE BEFORE TAKING YOUR IRA DISTRIBUTION...

Source: **Edward Mendlowitz, CPA,** partner, Mendlowitz Weitsen, LLP, CPAs, Two Pennsylvania Plaza, Suite 1500, New York 10121. He is author of eight books on taxes, including *IRA Distributions: What You Should Know.* Practical Programs, Inc.

For many people, an IRA will be their main source of retirement income. They want the funds to last as long as possible while at the same time generating a reasonable amount of income.

Others don't need the income. They want to take out as little as possible and keep the IRA going forever for the benefit of their heirs.

No matter what your IRA goals are, to achieve them you must make the right decisions before the money starts coming out. Decisions you'll have to make...

BENEFICIARIES...

If you haven't already done so, be sure to name a beneficiary who will inherit your IRA. Depending on your choice of beneficiary, this action may also reduce the amounts you're required by law to take from your IRA.

• *Name your spouse* if you believe that the funds from the IRA will be needed for his/her support after your death.

• *Name your children or grandchildren* to reduce your required minimum distributions—assuming your spouse doesn't need the money...or you no longer have a spouse.

• *Name a charity* to reduce your estate taxes. While naming a charity may increase your required minimum distributions at age 70½, this may not be a problem if you want the money for support.

While you can generally change beneficiaries at any time until you die, once required minimum distributions commence, you cannot alter the annual payouts even if you do change beneficiaries.

• *Name contingent—or alternative—beneficiaries.* What happens to your IRA in the event that your designated beneficiary dies before you?

If you haven't named an alternative beneficiary, the balance remaining in your IRA at your death will pass into your estate, requiring a more rapid distribution than if it had passed to another individual. Be sure to name an alternative.

EXAMPLE: You name your spouse as 100% beneficiary of your IRA. But if your spouse dies before you, then you name your two children each as 50% beneficiaries of your IRA. That way, your children, not your estate, will receive the IRA.

Naming an alternative beneficiary does not change the minimum distributions you're required to take after age 70½. The required distributions are determined solely with reference to you and your primary beneficiary—your spouse.

• *Divide your IRAs into separate accounts.* While you can name multiple beneficiaries to a single IRA, you obtain greater flexibility by dividing your funds among multiple IRAs. **THIS ALLOWS YOU TO...**

• Determine different distribution methods for each account.

• Name different beneficiaries to each account.

• Give your beneficiaries greater control over their inheritances. When you divide your IRAs, it is advisable to use a direct trustee-to-trustee transfer method (where the money never comes into your hands) rather than taking a distribution and rolling the funds over into one or more new IRAs.

FORMS...

• *You may need customized forms.* The forms provided by your IRA custodian to name beneficiaries and select distribution methods may not be sufficient for your purposes.

EXAMPLE: The forms may not allow you to name alternative beneficiaries, so work with a tax professional and your IRA custodian to develop forms that will meet your needs.

• *Keep good records.* Don't rely on banks, brokerage firms and other IRA custodians to retain the forms you've signed for your IRAs.

These forms cover your beneficiary designations and your distribution methods.

If you (or your family) can't prove your selections, then the custodian may apply default provisions that are counter to your wishes.

Before you even start to take your first distribution, be sure to obtain copies of necessary forms.

If the IRA custodian cannot find them—execute new ones and retain copies with your other important papers.

DISTRIBUTION METHODS...

• *Choose the right distribution method.* The law allows you to start taking money out of your IRA without penalty after you turn age 59½.

There are two main distribution methods that are used to figure out how much you can take out each year and still keep the IRA going for you and/or your surviving spouse. Those two methods are the *recalculation method* and the *term-certain method...*

• The recalculation method allows you to minimize your required lifetime distributions, but it can accelerate required distributions after your death.

• The term-certain method provides slightly larger required lifetime distributions but allows your beneficiaries to continue distributions at the same rate after your death.

Discuss these options with a financial planner and a tax professional before deciding which method to use.

CAUTION: If you fail to make a choice of methods, then the IRA trustee or custodian will apply its default method (generally the term-certain method).

• *Decide which IRA to take distributions from.* If you have more than one IRA, and you are age 70½ or older, you must figure your required minimum distribution for the year by adding your account balances together. But once you determine the required amount or if you're under age 70½, you can then take distributions from one or more.

In deciding which accounts to draw down first, consider...

• Investment performance of the accounts. Review the performance and project future returns. Generally, you'll want to draw down the account that's performing the least satisfactorily and let your money grow in the better-performing accounts.

• Which beneficiaries are named to which accounts. If you've named a different child as the beneficiary of each of your accounts, you'll probably want to draw down each account equally to preserve each of their equal shares.

REQUIRED DISTRIBUTIONS...

• *Figure the year in which you must begin to take distributions.* Age 70½ is the critical date for determining when you must start taking money from your traditional IRAs. This is so whether you're still working or have already retired. Believe it or not, failing to commence required distributions can result in a whopping 50% penalty.

NOTE: There are no mandatory withdrawals from Roth IRAs. You can continue to fund or simply leave money in Roth IRAs throughout your life.

WHEN TO TAKE THE FIRST REQUIRED DISTRIBUTION: The law allows you to take your first required distribution as late as April 1 of the year following the year of attaining age 70½.

TRAP: Waiting until this date means you'll have to take two distributions in the same year—the first distribution by April 1 and the second distribution by December 31 of the same year.

Delay distributions if you anticipate falling into a lower tax bracket in the year following attainment of age 70½.

EXAMPLE: You were born on April 1, 1930, and will retire at the end of 2000. Since you won't have any salary in 2001, you might want to delay your first distribution until after this year (but no later than April 1, 2001).

But if you expect that your income from your IRA and pension from your job will approximate your salary, then it may be in your best interests to take your first distribution by December 31, 2000. That way you won't be bunching two distributions into 2001.

401(K) PLAN TRAP

Source: **Terry Savage**, author, *The Savage Truth on Money* (John Wiley & Sons) and a syndicated *Chicago Sun-Times* financial columnist.

If you borrow funds from your 401(k) retirement account and leave your employer before repaying the loan, the entire outstanding balance will be taxable income to you. If you are under age 59½, it will be subject to an early distribution penalty as well.

SELF-DEFENSE: If you plan to retire or leave your employer and have 401(k) loans outstanding, repay them before you leave.

Whenever you take out a 401(k) loan, be aware of the tax risk should you leave your employer unexpectedly.

MUCH LONGER LIVES REQUIRE
MUCH SHREWDER RETIREMENT PLANNING

Source: **Ruth L. Hayden,** a financial educator and consultant based in St. Paul. She is author of *For Richer, Not Poorer: The Money Book for Couples.* Health Communications Inc.

When the Social Security system was established in 1935, people, on average, lived to the ripe old age of 62.

Today, thanks to advances in medicine, greater awareness of the benefits of good nutrition and an increased awareness of the benefits of physical exercise, we can expect to live as long as 30 years beyond retirement age—into our 80s and 90s.

To avoid financial mishaps during these bonus retirement years requires careful planning. You must keep yourself healthy emotionally, physically, mentally *and* financially. **TAKE TIME NOW TO...**

- *Imagine your future.*
- *Plan how you want to live.*
- *Practice making—and sticking to—a financial budget.*

SETTING GOALS...

Resolve any fears you may have for your financial future by setting retirement goals. **TO START...**

- *Write down what you want* to have...to do...to be...and to see during your retirement years. Ask yourself the following questions...

- What is my life going to be like emotionally, physically, mentally and financially?

- How will I continue to feel worthwhile and valuable to society?

- Will I continue working part-time or volunteer for a charity?

- Will I take care of my health by exercising regularly and eating a healthful diet?

- Do I have adequate health insurance?

- What will my finances be like in retirement?

This goal-setting stage of planning is the time to fantasize and dream about the future. Do you want to travel? Move to a different place? Spend more time with your grandchildren?

Launch your own business or a new career? Take up a new sport or hobby?

Whatever it is you want to do in retirement, write it all down.

• *Create a time frame for achieving your goals,* and write that down along the left-hand margin of a piece of paper.

Look at a calendar of years to come and choose actual dates by which each goal will be achieved. For every date, write down the age you'll be at that time.

• *Fit the hopes and dreams you wrote down in Step One* into the time frame you created in Step Two.

EXAMPLE: Make a column to the right of your "future dates" that asks, "What do I want?"

Then, add another column next to that one that asks, "What will I need to do by this date to make this goal happen?"

LESS MONEY...

The steps you need to take to accomplish your goals may or may not involve the accumulation of money.

No matter what they involve, however, write them down. When you've got a clear picture of what you want to achieve during your retirement years, create a budget that helps you both achieve your goals and get used to the idea of living on a reduced income.

Most of us will find ourselves living on a reduced—if not fixed—income at some time during our three-decade-long retirement. By setting a budget now and sticking to it, you'll know that you can do it. You can trust yourself to plan your finances and, by extension, plan your life.

Software packages can help you create a budget. My favorite is Intuit's *Quicken*. If you need additional help, read a book on budgeting and/or talk to a financial planner.

BUDGETING...

Things you'll want to take into account when creating a budget include...

• *Monthly fixed expenses.* Rent/mortgage, phone service, TV, Internet service, electric service, car payments, etc.

• *Nonmonthly fixed expenses.* Quarterly water service, car insurance payments, estimated taxes, etc.

• *Weekly flexible expenses.* Eating out, books, newspapers.

• *Nonmonthly optional expenses.* Gifts, theater tickets, movies, trips, etc.

The budget is your first step to financial security. You'll feel more in control of your finances, now and in the future, when you have your budget in place.

THE FUTURE...

To help carry that sense of financial control forward into retirement, adopt the following model for planning and managing your finances.

As circumstances such as health and living arrangements change, adapt the model and your financial plan to address your needs.

• *Between the ages of 60 and 70,* continue accumulating money for retirement. Take a part-time job and use the money you earn for cash-flow needs—buying groceries, paying bills, etc.

If your part-time job offers a 401(k) plan, take advantage of it. Otherwise, invest money in a traditional IRA, a Roth IRA and/or the stock market.

• *Between the ages of 70 and 80,* your health-care costs may go up. You may have quit working altogether. To continue living comfortably, use the income from your investments, but—if at all possible—don't touch the principal. If you do, your money may not hold out.

• *In life's later years, from the age of 80 on up,* do whatever you need to do financially to maintain autonomy and make your life work.

This is the time to dip into the principal, if necessary, from your investments and enjoy yourself!

■

FINANCING A RETIREMENT HOME

Source: **Maureen Tsu, CFP**, San Juan Capistrano, CA, quoted in *Where to Retire*, 1502 Augusta Dr., Suite 415, Houston 77057.

When buying a retirement home, a key decision is whether to purchase it with cash or finance it with a mortgage.

Many people prefer the security of buying with cash and not owing any debt on their home.

DRAWBACK: Using so much cash may leave you *cash poor* and limit the lifestyle you can afford in retirement.

CONTRAST: Buying a home with a mortgage can leave you with more spendable cash. The debt on the home can be paid off or refinanced upon your death.

Issues if you decide to finance with a mortgage...

• *Can you obtain tax benefits from deducting mortgage interest?* Do you have enough total deductions to itemize deductions? Are you in a high enough tax bracket to make it worthwhile?

• *Can you invest the cash saved* by buying with a mortgage to earn a higher after-tax rate of return than you will pay on the mortgage?

• *Are you willing to have your estate deal with the debt on your home* by selling it, or by having heirs refinance it at your death?

Issues if you buy with cash...

• *Will you have a way of tapping your equity in the home* to raise cash in an emergency?

• *After spending cash on the home,* will you have enough money to enjoy a comfortable retirement lifestyle?

• *Will your estate eventually sell the home for cash*—so that you might as well take the cash while you are alive by financing the home?

BEST: Consider these issues before you retire, while you are still working. You will have more options and a stronger credit standing to make any arrangement you finally choose.

■

TAX-FREE INCOME

Source: **Ed Slott, CPA**, E. Slott & Co., CPAs, 100 Merrick Rd., Suite 200E, Rockville Centre, NY 11570. *www.irahelp.com.* Mr. Slott is editor and publisher of *Ed Slott's IRA Advisor.*

Roth IRAs are being underused because many people's tax perspective is too short term.

Contributions to Roth IRAs aren't deductible, as they are with traditional IRAs, and conversions of traditional IRAs to Roth IRAs are taxable. But the benefits of a Roth IRA may far outweigh the current tax cost.

HOW: Future Roth IRA distributions are tax free. This alone may more than offset the initial tax in the long run.

In addition, Roth IRAs have no minimum distribution requirements, offer opportunities to make highly tax-favored bequests and allow contributed funds to be withdrawn tax and penalty free before age 59½.

Don't miss big future tax benefits for fear of incurring a smaller current tax cost.

■

WORKING PAST AGE 65

Source: **Barbara Weltman**, an attorney practicing in Millwood, NY. She is author of *The Complete Idiot's Guide to Making Money After You Retire*. Alpha Books.

Today, as people stay healthier and more active, many choose to work past the retirement age fixed by Social Security—age 65. That age will rise in stages to age 67 by 2027.

The decision to keep working may be motivated by...

• *A continuing need to earn income* because retirement savings, pensions and Social Security benefits won't ensure a comfortable retirement.

• *The enjoyment and fulfillment a person gets from having a job.*

IMPACT ON SOCIAL SECURITY BENEFITS...

If you're *under* age 65 and have already started collecting Social Security benefits, you may be in for a double whammy.

First, the amount of benefits you receive will be reduced because you've started collecting benefits before the normal retirement age.

Second, if you earn more than a certain income limit from a job or self-employment, your benefits are further reduced.

REDUCTION SCHEDULE: For every $2 over a threshold amount ($10,080 in 2000), you'll lose $1 in benefits.

BOTTOM LINE: Unless you have to retire early for health reasons or don't need your benefits for a secure retirement, it may pay to wait until your Social Security retirement age before collecting benefits.

True, starting early means more years of receiving benefits. But the reductions may just be too great if you continue to work.

If you're age 65 to 69, there's good news. Congress has recently agreed to end the earnings limit for Social Security ($17,000 for 2000), so working at this age won't affect your benefits.

Even better, if you already had your benefits cut in 2001, you'll receive a refund from Social Security retroactive to January 1, 2000.

WHAT TO DO: If you've already made arrangements for a reduced work schedule, it may be time to revisit the situation. If you want to work more and your employer is willing, then do so without concern about loss of Social Security benefits.

If you're age 70 and older, there has never been an earnings limit. Work as much as you want and collect benefits at the same time.

BONUS: As you continue to work, you may be increasing the benefits to which you are entitled. This is because benefits are figured on the most recent years' earnings. So as you work and earn, your benefits can be adjusted.

DOWNSIDE: Regardless of age, all earnings from a job or self-employment continue to be subject to Social Security (up to a threshold amount—$76,200 in 2000) and Medicare (without limit) taxes.

AGE DISCRIMINATION...

For the most part, you can't be denied a job, a promotion or any job-related benefits solely because of your age...though there are some very limited exceptions.

This means if you want to work, it's your right under the law.

Of course, this doesn't automatically guarantee you a job. As a practical matter, older workers may find younger workers are hired more readily than they are.

However, with the increasingly tight job market, older workers may be able to find the work they want.

If you think you've been discriminated against because of age, contact the Equal Employment Opportunity Commission (EEOC) at 800-669-4000 or *www.eeoc.gov*. This government agency may be able to press a claim on your behalf.

If you're not satisfied with government action, consider initiating a lawsuit against the employer who discriminated against you. Under federal law—*Age Discrimination in Employment Act (ADEA)*—those over age 40 can't be discriminated against on the basis of age by an employer who regularly has 20 or more workers. But ADEA won't help if...

• The employer is small (has fewer than 20 workers). Small employers are exempt from ADEA.

• You're an independent contractor who has been denied a contract on the basis of age. ADEA only protects employees and prospective employees.

• You served in a high policy-making position for at least two years before retirement and receive a substantial pension. Then compulsory retirement at age 70 isn't discriminatory.

NOTE: Most states also have their own laws against age discrimination.

IF YOU'RE DISABLED...

Under another federal law—*Americans with Disabilities Act*—employers who regularly employ at least 15 workers are prohibited from discriminating against a person on the basis of a disability when it comes to making employment-related decisions (hiring, firing, promotions, job assignments, benefits, etc.). What's more, these employers must make reasonable accommodations for a worker's disability as long as it doesn't place an undue hardship on the business.

Age alone isn't considered a disability. However, certain medical conditions associated with advanced age may be a disability, such as arthritis or osteoporosis. Then reasonable accommodations must be made to enable a person to work.

You can't be asked about a disability during the hiring process. You can only be questioned about your ability to do the job. Once you have the job, then you can ask that reasonable accommodations be made to help you do the work required.

HEALTH INSURANCE...

For many older workers, health coverage is a prime reason for continuing employment.

No employer is required to provide coverage for its workforce. But if it does, then you must receive benefits regardless of age. Once you're age 65 and entitled to Medicare, you're doubly protected. Your employer coverage usually is your primary payor, with Medicare as your secondary payor. Whatever your employer insurance fails to cover, Medicare may then pay.

CHOICE: While employers must offer you coverage, you can choose to reject it, letting Medicare become your primary payor.

WHY: You might consider rejecting employer coverage if you're paying for it. It may be cheaper to rely solely on Medicare.

PENSIONS...

Working past the normal retirement age can be an advantage in terms of retirement benefits.

You continue to participate in your employer's retirement plan and build up retirement benefits while you work.

Even if you're hired after the normal retirement age of your new employer's plan, you can't be excluded from participating in that plan.

If you're still working and reach age 70½ , you don't have to begin required minimum distributions from the *company's retirement plan*. You can postpone commencing minimum distributions until you eventually retire from the job.

However, even if you're working, distributions must commence from your IRAs no later than April 1 of the year following the year in which you reach age 70½.

■

TAX SMARTS

GIFT TAX VS. ESTATE TAX

Source: **David S. Rhine, CPA**, partner and national director of family wealth planning, BDO Seidman, LLP, 330 Madison Ave., New York 10017.

Gift tax is cheaper than estate tax. It is much less costly tax-wise to give property away and pay gift tax on it than to die owning the property and pay estate tax. This is so even though gift and estate taxes nominally apply at the same rate.

REASON: Gifts are made with before-tax dollars. But bequests are made with after-tax dollars, so more tax applies to the same-size transfer.

EXAMPLE: You are in the 55% gift and estate tax bracket. A gift of $100,000 results in gift tax of $55,000. But a bequest of $100,000 requires assets of $222,000 to have $100,000 left after taxes. The estate tax is $122,000, compared with gift tax of only $55,000 on a same-size after-tax transfer.

■

LIVING TOGETHER VS. MARRIAGE

Source: **Edward Mendlowitz, CPA**, partner, Mendlowitz Weitsen, LLP, CPAs, Two Pennsylvania Plaza, Suite 1500, New York 10121. He is author of several books on taxes, including *IRA Distributions: What You Should Know*. Practical Programs, Inc.

While Congress struggles to eliminate the penalty that requires married couples to pay more tax than single couples, more and more people are opting to live together rather than marry.

Cohabitation without the benefit of marriage is especially favored by older persons who want to protect their separate financial lives. **ISSUES OF IMPORTANCE FOR SINGLES INCLUDE...**

• *The right to collect Social Security benefits based on the earnings of a former spouse.*

• *The cessation of alimony payments upon remarriage.*

If you've chosen not to marry, consider the issues outlined below.

LIFETIME ISSUES...

• *Own your home in joint names.* If you do this as *tenants in common*, then each person has his/her own separate interest in the home. Upon death, that interest passes to heirs according to the terms of a will.

So, if you want your share of a home held as tenants in common to pass to your partner, you'll have to put that desire in your will.

If you own the home as *joint tenants with right of survivorship*, then upon the death of the first owner, the survivor automatically becomes the owner of the entire property.

The entire value of the home is included in the estate of the first owner to die, except to the extent the other paid for the home.

The portion of the home that's inherited gets a stepped-up basis—that is, its tax cost to the beneficiary is increased to the home's value on the date of the decedent's death.

From an income tax perspective, if you sell a jointly owned home, you *each* qualify for an income tax exclusion of up to $250,000 of profits from the home's sale. *Requirement:* You both must have owned and lived in the home for a total of at least two years out of the past five.

• *Cover your partner's medical costs.* Many employers today offer coverage for "domestic partners."

Find out what's required to obtain this status under the employer's medical plan so that you can provide employer-sponsored health coverage for your partner.

CAUTION: The employee is taxed on employer-paid medical coverage for a domestic partner. Only such coverage for a spouse is tax free.

If you support your partner, you may claim any medical costs paid on his behalf as a deductible itemized medical expense.

This is the case even if your partner doesn't qualify as your dependent because his gross income is more than the limit ($2,800 in 2001).

• *Authorize your partner to speak for you in a medical crisis*—to make medical decisions on your behalf.

WHAT TO DO: Sign a health-care proxy or other state-recognized document to name your partner as your agent for health-care purposes.

• *Authorize your partner to act for you in financial matters.* If an illness or medical condition prevents you from managing your financial affairs, empower your partner to act for you.

WHAT TO DO: Sign a durable power of attorney specifying that your partner can handle your money.

Make sure the power of attorney form allows your partner to act on tax matters. The IRS generally requires an agent to be appointed on IRS Form 2848, *Power of Attorney and Declaration of Representative.* But the IRS says it will let an agent act if he's been appointed under your own durable power of attorney.

BUSINESS-RELATED ISSUES...

• *Set up a business with your partner.* When you own a business together, you must plan for contingencies—retirement, disability, death or a parting of the ways. Like any other co-owners, you should have a buy-sell agreement to spell out what happens when these events transpire. **THERE ARE TWO TYPES OF BUY-SELL AGREEMENTS...**

• *Cross-purchase agreements* in which each owner agrees to buy out the interest of the departing owner.

• *Entity purchase (redemption) agreements* in which the business agrees to acquire the interest of the departing owner.

Generally, when there are only two owners, the cross-purchase agreement is used.

CAUTION: Use life insurance or another funding mechanism to ensure you have the money to follow through on the agreement's terms.

• *Hire your partner.* If you own a business, employ your partner. Salary paid for work performed is deductible by the business.

BREAK: If your partner isn't your dependent, his earnings are tax free if his total income is less than $7,200 ($8,300 if he's 65 or older).

ESTATE PLANNING ISSUES...

• *Give property to your partner.* While only marrieds have an unlimited marital deduction, you can still transfer property to your partner without any tax cost. You can give up to $10,000 each year gift tax free.

You can give even more tax free if you use your lifetime estate tax exemption amount ($675,000 in 2001, rising to $1 million by 2006). But any exemption amount used during your lifetime reduces the amount available for your estate.

• *Name your partner as beneficiary of your...*
• Company retirement benefits.
• IRAs.
• Life insurance.
• Annuities.

Since these assets pass directly to a named beneficiary outside of your probate estate, your relatives generally can't challenge these bequests.

BONUS: By naming a beneficiary to your IRA and company retirement benefits, you reduce the required lifetime distributions from these plans. Distributions will be computed on the basis of the joint life expectancy of you and your partner. If your partner is younger than you, the required minimum distributions are even smaller. *Note:* No matter how young your partner is, for distribution computation purposes, he's considered to be no more than 10 years your junior.

Generally, you retain the right to change a beneficiary designation until your death, but can't alter the payouts after age 70½, when required minimum distributions begin.

• *Protect bequests to your partner.* You can name your partner as an heir under the terms of your will. Alternatively, you can place your property in a trust and name your partner as a beneficiary of the trust. Generally, it's harder for relatives to contest the terms of a trust than to upset a will.

Property passing to your partner—by will or under the terms of a trust—does not qualify for the unlimited marital deduction, even if he's your domestic partner. But your estate can use your lifetime exemption amount to shield bequests to your partner from estate tax.

• *Name your partner your executor.* You can make sure your estate is handled the way you want and provide money for your partner by naming him an executor (or co-executor) of your estate. Executors are entitled to fees for their services in administering an estate.

■

VERY BIG OVERLOOKED TAX DEDUCTION

Source: **Ed Slott, CPA**, E. Slott & Co., CPAs, 100 Merrick Rd., Ste. 200E, Rockville Centre, NY 11570. *www.irahelp.com.* Mr. Slott is editor and publisher of *Ed Slott's IRA Advisor.*

Many people who inherit IRAs overlook a potentially big tax deduction—that for "income in respect of a decedent."

KEY: A bequeathed IRA may be subject to double taxation—first estate tax, then income tax when its proceeds are distributed. Combined, these two taxes may total 70% or more.

SAVER: To soften the blow when inherited assets are subject to both estate and income tax in this way, those who inherit the assets can take an income tax deduction for the federal estate tax paid on the assets. And for IRAs that hold a lifetime of retirement savings, this deduction may be huge.

EXAMPLE: If you inherit an IRA worth $200,000, the federal estate tax on it may be $80,000—entitling you to claim $80,000 of income tax deductions over the period during which you withdraw money from the IRA.

TRAP: Many people don't take this deduction at all, simply because they don't know about it. Don't let this happen in your family. Whether you are likely to bequeath an IRA or inherit one, ask your tax adviser about the rules for "income in respect of a decedent"—and plan accordingly.

■

VERY TAX-WISE WAYS TO HELP YOUR GRANDCHILDREN

Source: **Edward Mendlowitz, CPA**, partner, Mendlowitz Weitsen, LLP, CPAs, Two Pennsylvania Plaza, Suite 1500, New York 10121. He is author of several books on taxes, including *IRA Distributions: What You Should Know*. Practical Programs, Inc.

Grandparents who are in a financial position to help out their grandchildren may be rewarded for doing so with special tax breaks. **WAYS TO BE OF HELP...**

1. *Pay for college.* **OPTIONS...**

• Fund a Qualified State Tuition Plan (QSTP). Most states now offer some form of qualified tuition plan that allows you to contribute on behalf of your grandchild. If you're married—and your spouse consents to the gift—gifts up to $100,000 can be fully tax free. **HERE'S HOW...**

You can elect on a gift tax return to treat the $100,000 as having been made over five years. You won't pay gift tax because $100,000 spread equally over five years is $20,000 a year, and that's the maximum amount you and your spouse can jointly give a grandchild annually without owing gift tax.

IMPACT: The estate tax savings potential to you is enormous if you have several grandchildren and can afford to make this gift to each.

BONUS FOR SOME: You may be entitled to a state income tax deduction for a portion of your contribution.

• Contribute to an education IRA. Depending on your Adjusted Gross Income, you may be able to put up to $500 per year per grandchild into one of the new education IRAs. Your grandchild isn't taxed on contributions you make to the IRA, nor on the earnings on the contributions. And—withdrawals for qualified education costs are tax free.

• Pay tuition directly to the school. You can pay tuition for grandchildren or other relatives of any age, in any amount, directly to the school at no gift tax cost to you. This gift tax benefit is in addition to the annual gift tax exclusion of $10,000 ($20,000 for a married couple who join in making the gift).

2. Pay medical expenses. Like direct payments of tuition to schools, direct payments of medical expenses on behalf of a grandchild are exempt from gift tax.

3. Make interest-free loans. As a general rule, if a lender fails to charge interest of at least the applicable federal rate (AFR) —an interest rate set by the IRS and published monthly on *www.irs.gov*—then the lender must report "imputed interest income." This is the interest that would have been earned using the AFR rate.

EXCEPTIONS: There's no imputed interest income on loans of up to $10,000. And loans up to $100,000 are free of imputed income if the grandchild's net investment income (investment income minus investment expenses) is $1,000 or less.

If net investment income is more, then imputed interest charged *to you* is limited to the extent of your grandchild's net investment income.

4. Make grandchildren beneficiaries of your IRAs and pensions. When you die, amounts remaining in your plans will belong automatically to your grandchildren.

Naming a grandchild as beneficiary will allow you to reduce your required post-70½ minimum distributions from the plan.

When you name your grandchild as beneficiary, you can figure your minimum annual distributions based on the longer joint life expectancy of you and your beneficiary/grandchild, minimizing payouts.

5. Transfer assets to grandchildren. By giving assets to them you may be able to turn income that would be taxable to you at your high tax rate into tax-free income to the grandchildren. Income earned by your grandchildren on the assets may be shielded by their income tax exemption or taxed at their low rates.

• If your grandchild is under age 14, then he/she can receive investment income up to $700 tax free in 2001.

The next $700 of investment income of a child under age 14 is taxed at 15%. Investment income over $1,400 is taxed to the grandchild at his parents' top income tax rate.

• If he is 14 or older, he can have investment income up to $700 tax free. Investment income over this amount is taxed at the grandchild's tax rates. For 2001, up to $26,250 is taxed at only 15%.

• If he is taxed at the 15% rate on regular income, the rate he pays on capital gains is only 10%.

OPPORTUNITY: Starting in 2001, capital gains are subject to only an 8% tax for those in the 15% bracket—on assets held more than five years.

Assets acquired by gift include the donor's holding period, so if you give appreciated stock you've owned for more than five years and your grandchild sells it in 2001, the top tax on the gain will be only 8%.

6. *Set up custodial accounts.* Even if your grandchild is just a baby, you can start him off with savings through the use of gifts to custodial accounts. You can set up these accounts with banks, brokerage firms or mutual funds under the *Uniform Transfers (or Gifts) to Minors Act*. Use these accounts to put money aside for your grandchild.

Since the grandchild's Social Security number is on the account, the income is taxed to him under the rules discussed above—the under 14 years of age, over 13 rules.

CAUTION I: Don't act as the account's custodian yourself. Doing so can result in the money being included in your estate when you die, even though the funds are owned by your grandchild.

CAUTION II: Before you give money to your grandchild, consider the impact it might have on college financial aid he may be entitled to later on. Funds in a grandchild's name count heavily against grants of aid.

7. *Set up a trust fund.* If you want to give substantial assets to your grandchild, it's generally wise to use a trust. This will provide greater control over assets. As long as the trust meets certain requirements, gifts to the trust will qualify for the annual gift tax exclusion even though the grandchild can't touch the money immediately.

CAUTION: Consult a tax expert to ensure that the trust is a Section 2503(b) or Section 2503(c) trust. These are special trusts endorsed by the Tax Code that allow money put into the trust to qualify for the annual gift tax exclusion.

8. *Use life insurance.* Give your grandchild substantial amounts through life insurance. If your child doesn't need the money (he's already got an estate of his own), consider naming a grandchild as beneficiary of your life insurance policy.

If the policy is owned by a trust that's properly set up, your estate will escape tax on the proceeds.

CAUTION: Consider the impact of the generation-skipping transfer tax.

9. *Bring your grandchildren into the business.* You can provide income to your grandchildren while reducing your estate on favorable tax terms. **HERE'S ONE WAY...**

Set up a Family Limited Partnership (FLP). Transfer stocks, real estate or other appreciated assets into the company. Give interests in the FLP to your grandchildren at a discount to the value of the underlying assets of about 30%.

10. *Put business assets in a trust fund for your grandchildren.* If your business is about to buy an asset, consider setting up a trust to buy the asset. Make your grandchild the trust beneficiary and have the business lend the trust the funds to buy the asset.

Charge the trust the AFR to avoid gift tax issues. *Result:* The grandchild will obtain the benefit of the asset's future appreciation—which will be kept out of your estate.

VARIATION: Instead of using a trust, the same objectives can be accomplished through an FLP.

■

VACATION HOME TAX SAVINGS

Source: **Lisa N. Collins, CPA/PFS**, vice president and director of tax services, Harding, Shymanski & Co., PC, Box 3677, Evansville, IN 47735.

Tax law now allows up to $250,000 of gain to be taken tax free on the sale of a home that you've lived in for at least two of the prior five years. On a joint return, $500,000 can be taken tax free.

OPPORTUNITY: Many people also own a second home— either as a vacation home or a property that they rent out for income. In either case, if the second home has appreciated in value, after selling the first home the owner can move into the second home and two years later sell it for a tax-free gain, too.

RESULT: A married couple could take as much as $1 million of tax-free gain in just over two years.

■

HAVING SEVERAL IRAs

Source: **Ed Slott, CPA**, E. Slott & Co., CPAs, 100 Merrick Rd., Ste. 200E, Rockville Centre, NY 11570. *www.irahelp.com.* Mr. Slott is editor and publisher of *Ed Slott's IRA Advisor.*

You can own as many IRA accounts as you want. And for most people, it is a good idea to have more than one—probably several.

Having multiple IRAs can help you keep funds in them longer …to earn more tax-deferred investment returns…meet family financial planning goals…reduce estate taxes…and attain other valuable objectives.

IRA FLEXIBILITY...

Multiple IRAs can greatly increase your flexibility in managing your IRA wealth. **KEYS...**

• *Each IRA can have different beneficiaries.*

• *After reaching age 70½, your total minimum required annual distribution from all your IRAs can be taken from any one of them*—leaving the other IRAs intact.

• *You can transfer funds between IRAs without any negative consequences* until you begin taking required distributions at age 70½.

You can use these rules to get the most from your IRA savings and maximize family wealth. **HOW TO DO IT...**

• *Preserve funds for children.* When one spouse inherits an IRA from the other, the surviving spouse can place the inherited funds in a *new* IRA set up for this purpose instead of rolling them over into his/her existing IRA. By doing so—and by naming children or grandchildren as beneficiaries of the new IRA—current minimum required distributions may be reduced... and decades worth of tax-deferred IRA earnings may be saved for the children.

EXAMPLE: Two spouses are both over age 70½, and each owns an IRA. Each has named the other as his IRA beneficiary and is taking minimum annual distributions under the "recalculation" method.

If one spouse dies, the survivor can place inherited IRA funds into either his existing IRA or into a newly created IRA.

IF THE FUNDS GO INTO...

• The surviving spouse's existing IRA, they must be distributed at a rate based on the spouse's remaining life expectancy —for instance, about 10 years for a 79-year-old. When that spouse dies, all the funds in the IRA must be distributed and taxed within one year.

• A new IRA created by the surviving spouse with children named as beneficiaries, the funds may be distributed over the joint life expectancy of the spouse and beneficiaries. (Non-spouse beneficiaries are treated as no more than 10 years younger than the IRA owner regardless of actual age.)

RESULT: The payout period over which minimum annual distributions must be made is increased to 19 years from 10 years for a 79-year-old IRA owner. This reduces required annual distributions almost by half, leaving more funds in the IRA for the children to inherit.

When the children do inherit the new IRA, they can take distributions from it based on their own life expectancies, which may cover decades. They may receive 30 or 40 years (or more) of tax-deferred IRA earnings and distributions that would have been lost entirely had the second IRA not been created.

That's one benefit of establishing a new, separate IRA to hold the inherited funds—and there's also another.

After the surviving spouse establishes the new IRA, he will own two IRAs—his own old IRA, plus the new IRA with the children as beneficiaries.

The surviving spouse's minimum required annual distribution will be based on the combined balance in both IRAs. But he does not have to take distributions from both IRAs each year. In fact, doing so will deplete funds in the new IRA that benefits the children, while helping preserve the funds in the old IRA—which must be liquidated and taxed on the surviving spouse's death.

BETTER: The surviving spouse's full minimum required annual distribution can be taken from his own old IRA, leaving the new IRA untouched.

That way, only the old IRA that must be liquidated anyway on the surviving spouse's death is depleted—and the new IRA that benefits the children is left totally intact to grow for their benefit.

• *Flexibly provide for spouse and children.* Before reaching age 70½ you can divide your IRA assets into two IRAs, one with your spouse as beneficiary and the other one with a child as beneficiary.

Later, if your spouse seems adequately provided for (by insurance or otherwise), you can take all your IRA distributions from the IRA with your spouse as beneficiary to leave more for the children—who again may receive decades of benefits.

But if it seems your spouse may need extra funds, you can take all distributions from the IRA with the children beneficiaries to leave more for your spouse.

POINT: You can use the same strategy with several IRAs set up for children, grandchildren or other beneficiaries.

But if you don't create the separate IRAs, and it turns out your spouse won't need the IRA funds, you won't be able to flexibly shift IRA funds to the children or others in this manner—and a big opportunity may be lost.

• *Manage broad family bequests.* By setting up separate IRAs that each have a different child, grandchild or other person as beneficiary, you can fund each IRA with an appropriate amount for the beneficiary's particular needs.

EXAMPLE: You may place a smaller amount in an IRA with a grandchild as a beneficiary than in one with a child as a beneficiary, because of the extra years of IRA earnings that the younger grandchild will expect to receive.

TAX ADVANTAGE: By having a separate IRA for each beneficiary, each will be able to take future distributions from the IRA using his own life expectancy. In contrast, if you name several beneficiaries to a single IRA, all may be required to take distributions using the life expectancy of the oldest beneficiary—or else go through the potentially difficult process of breaking up the IRA into separate IRAs.

If the needs of your beneficiaries change over time, you can transfer funds among IRAs. After you begin taking IRA distributions, you can adjust the amount in each IRA by choosing which IRA you will take distributions from.

• *Take penalty-free early distributions.* If you have two or more IRAs, one of which was inherited, you have a special opportunity to take penalty-free early distributions.

KEY: The 10% penalty on distributions taken before age 59½ does not apply to funds in an IRA that you inherit as a beneficiary.

That's good enough—but with planning, you will be able to take funds from both IRAs before age 59½ without penalty.

HOW: Even if you are under age 59½, you will be required to take minimum IRA distributions due to your ownership of the inherited IRA funds. But you do not have to take them from the inherited IRA—you can take them from either IRA.

STRATEGY: Take the required distributions on the inherited IRA from your own IRA. Because distributions from an inherited IRA are required, they will be penalty free, even if taken from your own IRA. That will leave the funds in the inherited IRA untouched—and you can take all of them penalty free any time you wish.

PAYOFF: Each year you will find yourself with a larger amount accumulated in the inherited IRA—all of which you can withdraw at any time, penalty free.

• *Manage investments.* You may find it easier to fund different IRAs with different kinds of investments, depending on the particular investment expertise of different IRA trustees—such as banks, brokers, mutual fund companies, etc.

Before you begin taking required distributions, you can rebalance your portfolio periodically with IRA-to-IRA transfers.

After you start taking distributions, you can take all of them from one IRA with investments you want to liquidate...while leaving more promising investments in other IRAs intact.

■

TRAVEL AND LEISURE

FRESH THINKING ABOUT HANDLING MONEY WHEN YOU TRAVEL

Source: **Bob Howells**, correspondent for *Outside Magazine* and writer for *National Geographic Adventure*. He is author of *The RVer's Money Book*. Trailer Life Books.

Before you leave on a trip this winter, accommodations must be made to cover financial matters while you're away from home, especially if you plan to be gone for an extended period of time. Here are a few areas to consider...

• *Consolidate and simplify.* Arrange to have as few bills coming in as possible while you're away. *Helpful:* Limit the number of credit cards you carry.

EXAMPLE: Instead of carrying five gasoline credit cards in your wallet, pay for fuel using a single Visa or MasterCard.

Contact creditors about setting up automatic payment plans to pay regular monthly bills directly from your checking account. *Including:* Mortgage payments...utility bills...insurance premiums.

Arrange for direct deposit of regularly arriving checks. *Including:* Social Security...dividends...pension payments.

• *Have a trusted friend or family member pick up your mail.* Leave a supply of presigned checks so they can pay any unexpected bills that arrive. *Also:* Have them review your mail to make sure nothing important—such as a notice from the IRS—goes unanswered.

ALTERNATIVE: If you're going to be traveling on a schedule or will be in only one location, have your mail forwarded directly to you.

HOW: If you will be in only one location, have your local post office forward your mail. If you'll be moving around, contact a mail forwarding service—listed in the Yellow Pages (look under "Mail Receiving Services"). These services will receive your mail from the post office, bundle it up and forward it to you anywhere in the world. *Including:* To a private mailing address...a hotel...RV campsite office...post office general delivery.

• *Get an Automated Teller Machine (ATM) directory.* Contact your bank or ATM card network for a directory of locations. In the US, machines are easy to find, but in some countries, machines are tied into only one network.

ON THE ROAD...

Gaining access to your money when you're on the road can be a problem. There are several useful options...

• *Traveler's checks.* The old standby for travelers, traveler's checks are readily negotiable in an emergency—or when you are temporarily unable to find an ATM for some reason.

Carry—at most—only several hundred dollars in traveler's checks. *Reason:* You usually have to pay a 1% service charge, plus you'll tie up money that could otherwise be earning interest.

• *ATMs.* ATMs give you instant access to your money, and with so many available in the US and Canada, one is always nearby. Plus, more and more businesses are accepting ATM cards for purchases.

STRATEGY: Keep most of your funds in an interest-bearing checking or savings account linked to your ATM card so you'll continue to earn interest on your money until the day you withdraw it.

IMPORTANT: ATMs often charge transaction fees of $1 to $2 for network withdrawals, so compare charges when selecting a bank.

• *Credit cards.* A great convenience for travelers, credit cards eliminate the need to carry a lot of cash and allow you to "float" your money for as long as 60 days—the time from when you make a purchase to when you have to pay for it.

You may need to carry two credit cards. One for making purchases and the second for checking into hotels or renting cars.

BACKGROUND: When a hotel or car rental company makes an imprint of your card, a portion of your credit line is tied up as a security measure to cover damage to the room or car. It may be two to three weeks before that amount is released—usually only when payment is received from the card company.

PROBLEM: If you rent a few cars or stay in several hotel rooms, your credit limit can easily be exhausted, making the credit card worthless.

SELF-DEFENSE: Carry another emergency card or a charge card—such as American Express or Diner's Club—which has no credit limit. In an emergency, most credit cards can be used to withdraw cash from ATMs.

NOTE: These withdrawals—via credit card—are considered cash advances and begin accruing interest from the moment the money is withdrawn.

CASH-ADVANCE FEES: Most cards charge cash-advance withdrawal fees of up to 3% of the total amount withdrawn, not to exceed a maximum of $10 to $25.

• *Carry a telephone calling card.* Available from AT&T, MCI, Sprint and other long-distance providers, they let you bill telephone calls to a personal account, use the provider of your choice and avoid the exorbitant rates charged by no-name long-distance companies.

■

MONEY SAVERS

Source: The Mature Traveler, P.O. Box 15791, Sacramento, CA 95852.

There are 350 toy libraries around the US. You can even take grandkids along to pick out the toys they want to borrow. *For one near you:* Send a self-addressed, stamped, business-sized envelope to USA Toy Library Association, 1213 Wilmette Ave., Suite 201, Wilmette, Illinois 60091, or call 847-920-9030.

• *Travel for less—even for free.* Put together a travel group and lead it. Grand Circle Travel, 800-597-2452, and Vantage Deluxe World Travel, 800-634-2180, ext. 6107, help show you how to put groups together to earn free or discounted travel. Also, most major cruise lines will provide one free group leader ticket for a certain number of reservations—sometimes as few as 10.

■

ART—DUTY FREE

Source: **Shelly Meyers**, US Customs senior import specialist, Los Angeles.

Artworks can be brought through US Customs duty free from abroad.

SNAG: "Artworks" are what the US Customs office says they are. This includes original paintings, drawings, pastels and collages—as long as they were made entirely by hand—plus other art objects if the creator was trained as an artist, graduated from a recognized art institution or has exhibited his/her works in galleries or museums. So, you may need to be able to prove the status of the work's creator.

TRAP: Fine works created by craftsmen, such as glass works, don't necessarily qualify as artwork—although they are often sold as "duty free." If you are considering acquiring valuable works while traveling abroad, contact the nearest Customs office before leaving on your trip to learn the rules.

■

DIGITAL MUSIC FROM THE WEB

Easy to download to your computer, there are hundreds of thousands of CD-quality digitized songs available in a format called MP3. You can search music sites, download the songs, play them on your computer, load them onto a solid-state portable music player designed for MP3 and even record CDs. Check out *www.mp3.com* and *www.emusic.com*.

■

CONSUMER
SAVVY

BETTER PHONE SERVICE

Get the best deals on phone services via a new free Web site. Enter your ZIP code and type of service desired to anonymously request customized quotes from competing service providers in your area. Services include long-distance, wireless, data and Internet.

DETAILS: *www.simplexity.com* or call 800-429-1942.

■

GET BARGAIN AMTRAK FARES
FROM ITS WEB SITE

Every Monday, Amtrak's Rail SALE program offers fares of up to 70% off only through its Web site. Fares are available at least for a week between the two cities listed and intermediate destinations. It's possible to upgrade from coach seating on board, subject to availability. The Rail SALE Web page is at *http://reservations.amtrak.com/rs.html.*

■

CREDIT CARD SMARTS

Source: **Gerri Detweiler,** credit specialist and author of *Invest in Yourself: Six Secrets to a Rich Life.* John Wiley & Sons.

When you cancel a credit card, be sure it's listed as closed on your credit report. If the report still lists the account as open, your ability to borrow may be reduced. After canceling a card, ask for written verification that it has been canceled. A month later, ask for a copy of your credit report. If the report still shows the account as open, inform the credit bureau and send it a copy of the verification letter showing the account to be closed. By law, credit bureaus must verify disputed information with the source within 30 days.

■

SAVE ON VITAMINS

Source: **V. Srini Srinivasan, PhD**, director, dietary supplements division, US Pharmacopeia, 12601 Twinbrook Pkwy., Rockville, MD 20852.

Nearly all vitamin supplement makers buy their raw vitamins from the same suppliers.

Just three major manufacturers—Roche, BASF and Rhone-Poulenc—produce 90% of the world's vitamins. So, no matter which brand you buy or how much you pay, and regardless of the appearance of the vitamin pill, you are getting the same basic vitamin product. You can save a lot of money if you buy the drugstore's house brand.

CAUTION: How the raw vitamin is formulated for use—tablets, gel caps, capsules, etc.—can affect how well it dissolves in your body. Look for "USP" on the label to be sure the product meets US Pharmacopeia standards for dissolvability.

■

CUT THE COST OF PRESCRIPTION DRUGS

Source: Harvard Health Letter, 10 Shattuck St., Boston 02115.

B e willing to take medication several times a day—doctors often prescribe more expensive one-dose-per-day drugs, assuming patients prefer them.

Use medication as prescribed. When a patient fails to follow instructions—often because of unpleasant side effects—a drug may not work. Your doctor may then prescribe a more expensive substitute when it may be possible to adjust the inexpensive prescription you're already taking.

Buy generic rather than brand-name drugs when available. Shop around for the best deal—prices vary.

IMPORTANT: Ask your doctor to help. Doctors often don't worry about drug costs, assuming insurance covers them.

■

YARD SALE SAVVY

Source: **William Stratas**, owner, Garage Sale Promotions, 38 Elm St., Toronto, Ontario, Canada M5G 2K5.

C lean house thoroughly to decide what to sell. Sell as many things as possible. Include some unusual items—they can create interest in the whole sale. Set prices at reasonable levels, but allow negotiating room—buyers expect to bargain. Post large, easily readable signs on trees and utility poles nearby. To avoid having buyers return broken items, mark anything with a potential problem *as is* or *doesn't work.* Keep your sense of humor—yard sales should be fun.

■

PAY LESS FOR ATM USE

Source: **Laurie Berger**, editor, *Consumer Reports Travel Letter,* 101 Truman Ave., Yonkers, NY 10703.

T wo new Internet banking services offer free in-network and out-of-network use of ATMs—and help reimburse charges made by other banks.

• *Membership B@nking*, from American Express, gives a reimbursement of up to $1.50 per use on an interest-bearing checking account—maximum $6 per month—for out-of-network ATM use. There is no charge for using 8,700 American Express ATMs around the US. *More information:* 888-356-1006 or *www.americanexpress.com/banking*.

• *Wingspan Bank.com* gives a monthly rebate of up to $5 for out-of-network ATM use, with no per-transaction limit. Its ATM cards can be used free at 7,000 BankOne ATMs. *More information:* 888-736-8611 or *www.wingspanbank.com*.

■

BUSINESS SMARTS

GREAT WAYS TO CUT HOTEL COSTS

Source: **Christopher J. McGinnis**, director of Travel Skills Group, a communications and consulting firm specializing in the business travel industry, Box 52927, Atlanta 30355. He is author of *The Unofficial Business Travelers Pocket Guide.* McGraw-Hill.

Why not get a great hotel room for the same money, or less, than you'd pay for a standard room? Try these strategies I recommend to my business-traveler clients...

• *Consolidators.* National consolidators provide deep discounts. Try Quikbook (800-789-9887 or *www.quikbook.com*) ...Hotel Reservations Network (800-964-6835 or *www.hotel disconts.com*)...or Priceline (*www.priceline.com*).

EXAMPLE: The Beverly Plaza in Los Angeles charges $179 to $228 for a room...Quikbook's rate is $125.

DOWNSIDE: Some consolidators require advance payment.

BEWARE: Hotels that are "frayed around the edges" often unload rooms with consolidators. But some desirable properties—such as Chicago's Drake and Palmer House hotels—do work with consolidators. Know your hotels before you book.

- *Travel consortia.* Many travel agencies belong to networks that can provide discounts and upgrades. Leaders include Hickory Travel Systems (800-448-0349).

- *Be specific when you book a room.*

EXAMPLE: Nonsmoking, lake view, between floors three and 10, away from the pool, etc. This way, if the hotel can't meet your specifications, it might give you an upgrade.

- *Get out of the mainstream.* Check out lesser-known boutique hotels, such as those of...

- The Kimpton Hotel Group (no 800 number...call hotels individually, listed at *www.kimptongroup.com*) on the West Coast.

- Manhattan East Suite Hotels (800-637-8483 or *www. mesuite.com*).

- Boutique Hotels (877-847-4444...call hotels individually, listed at *www.boutiquehg.com*) in New York.

EXAMPLE: Boutique's five Manhattan properties are known for their stylish period designs and architectural integrity. They offer breakfast...dessert buffets...VCRs and CD players... libraries of videos and CDs—all free.

- *Use clout on the right people.* A couple of weeks before you leave, send a note to the manager of guest relations or the front-desk manager. Introduce yourself...suggest that you might be staying often...and that you might refer business.

When you get to the hotel, say hello to these people. You may get a better room or free breakfast. If you do, write a thank-you note.

- *Work the wiggle room.* Rates are not set in stone. Smoke out the lowest price in town, and ask the manager you've met to match it. Also, ask for the corporate rate *of the company that you are visiting.* Often the hotel has a local rate that only in-house reservationists are aware of. If you can't get a break on the room, ask for free upgrades—breakfast, valet services, transportation.

- *Call right after 6 pm.* This is when hotels wipe out all reservations unsecured by a credit card...and may offer rooms at a bargain rate. In high-occupancy cities—New York or San Francisco—many hotels have a 4 pm deadline.

- *Join the club*...a frequent-guest program will get you a few extras—and it costs nothing to join.

EXAMPLE: Starwood Preferred Guest Program offers Gold Preferred Guest Benefits...check cashing privileges, upgrades, late checkout and three star points per dollar spent toward a free night. For more information, call 888-625-4988.

■

HOW TO TAKE FULL ADVANTAGE OF THE AMAZING MONEY-RAISING OPPORTUNITIES TODAY

Source: **David R. Evanson**, investor relations consultant, Financial Communications Associates, Inc., 27 W. Athens Ave., Ardmore, PA 19003. He is author of *Where to Go When the Bank Says No*. Bloomberg Press.

Today there are more excellent options than ever to raise equity or borrow money. **KEY STEPS TO SUCCESS...**

• *Make your company appear to lenders as a well-established, growth-oriented winner.* That doesn't, of course, mean tampering with facts. It *does* entail assembling a competent team of the company's leaders, putting together thorough and professional financial projections and polishing your sales pitch.

• *Target only lenders or investors with track records of working with small companies.* Don't waste time knocking on doors of venture capitalists who are interested only in flashy start-ups and multimillion-dollar deals. And unless you've developed a cozy relationship with a loan officer, don't bother with banks, which are generally interested only in safe loans to companies with lots of assets.

Instead, go to the many new capital sources that have sprung up in the last few years—such as angel investors...online investment capital networks...new forms of venture capital ...private-placement firms.

WEARING STILTS...

Before approaching lenders or investors, make an effort to build up the company's image by...

• *Focusing on a lead investor.* This is either a well-known capital source or one who makes a large initial investment—or both. The real value is often in a lead investor's ability to attract other sources of capital.

• *Retaining legal counsel that knows the investment scene.* The move is not only prudent, but having a good attorney makes your business appear confident and professional in the eyes of many investors.

• *Lining up solid references.* The most impressive ones are potential customers—the people who will generate profits for your growing company.

When an investor asks about your potential customers, the last thing you want to say is, "I'll get back to you." Instead, hand him/her a list of three or four loyal customers and their phone numbers. Then say, "I'd really like you to call them."

BUSINESS PLAN TRAP...

A detailed business plan is essential for attracting investment capital, but it's only a first step.

REALITY: No one just reads a business plan and sends you a check. At best, a well-drafted plan will get you appointments with the right people and give them a broad picture of why you want the money.

CAUTION: An experienced business plan writer can produce a professional document and save you time. But when you hire a writer, you give up the discipline of thinking through each aspect of the plan yourself.

That lapse can be painfully conspicuous when you talk in person to an investor who has read the plan and has some tough follow-up questions that you don't really know the answers to—because you didn't write the plan.

SIMPLE SOLUTION: Write the plan yourself, and show it to members of your advisory team who have had experience in raising money. If necessary, consider hiring a professional writer to polish the plan.

HELPFUL: A deal summary of 200 to 500 words that lays out the venture appealingly, succinctly and without jargon. Use the summary when you have to give a quick overview of your plan.

To make sure investors can easily understand the opportunity that you're offering them, show the summary to advisers who aren't in your own industry. These people can often spot jargon or other terms that would confuse investors.

NEW MONEY SOURCES...

Banks usually don't lend to new businesses. Typically, new businesses lack a strong cash flow or assets that can be sold off in case of default. Banks also shy away from lending to small companies because processing a $500,000 loan costs the bank about as much as processing a $5 million loan, which is far more profitable.

More-productive sources of raising money...

• *ACE-Net and other private capital networks (PCNs).* PCNs link entrepreneurs with cash sources, usually via the Internet. Most are affiliated with a university or government development council, and as a group, they're revolutionizing the task of money raising for small businesses.

ACE-Net, which can be located on the Internet at *http:// ace-net.sr.unh.edu*, is perhaps the best of the PCNs. Cosponsored by the US Small Business Administration (SBA), Ace-Net works with the Securities & Exchange Commission and state regulators to match entrepreneurs with accredited investors —a distinction that weeds out small players who might not be knowledgeable about investing.

Among Ace-Net's advantages is a procedure for simplifying much of the legal work for money seekers. It's still prudent, however, to retain an attorney to look over legal forms as well as anything you post on the Internet concerning the company's search for funds.

The SBA also licenses—without endorsing—more than two dozen firms that lend to or invest in small companies. These firms can be located at *www.sba.gov*. Other PCNs can be located by keying in "capital private networks" in a search engine.

CAUTION: Since the Internet is open to anyone who has access to it, there are inevitably some less-than-ethical players.

RULE OF THUMB: Deal only with "closed" on-line organizations that at least take some steps to screen both the money-seeking companies and potential investors.

HOW TO IDENTIFY CLOSED SYSTEMS: Like Ace-Net, they have some combination of registration, screening and payment (usually less than $500). If *you* can access a PCN's Web site—it's not closed.

• *Business incubators.* These organizations, usually affiliated with universities and/or business associations, provide small companies with a location and resources designed to facilitate growth. Most are affiliated with sources of capital.

Incubators can be located through the Web site of the National Business Incubation Association, which is at *www.nbia.org*.

• *Venture capital clubs.* Often linked to universities or economic development authorities, these groups of wealthy investors exchange information and often pool their capital to make investments.

They typically screen business plans and invite selected entrepreneurs to make a pitch to members.

WHERE TO FIND THEM: Through business schools at major universities, chambers of commerce and Internet search engines.

• *Venture capital forums.* They're usually sponsored by local or regional universities or business groups. The objective is to foster growth of young companies by putting them in touch with professionals, including lenders and investors.

EXAMPLE: The Mid-Atlantic Venture Association, 2345 York Rd., Timonium, Maryland 21093, 410-560-5855, *www.mava.org*. Like many similar organizations, Mid-Atlantic offers small-business owners access to financing and joint-venture opportunities.

■

HOW TO OUT-MARKET THE BIG GUYS

Source: **Jay Levinson,** chairman, Guerrilla Marketing International, Box 1336, Mill Valley, CA 94942. He is author of several books, including *Mastering Guerrilla Marketing.* Houghton-Mifflin.

Big competitors with huge budgets can always be counted on to outspend their smaller rivals. But—that doesn't mean they always win.

Today, in fact, businesses of all sizes have more and more weapons in their arsenal for leveling the marketing playing field.

MOST EFFECTIVE NOW...

• *Zero in on best prospects.* Large companies often blanket an area with expensive catalogs or other direct mail.

DRAWBACK: Because it's a scattershot approach, the campaign reaches only a small number of consumers who actually are interested in the products or services.

The better—and much cheaper—alternative is to target only likely prospects. In the marketing business that's called "consent marketing." **EXAMPLES...**

• *Use inexpensive print ads to offer free catalogs or brochures to people who request them.* If you use brochures, include a toll-free telephone number for recipients to call for more information or for a visit from a sales representative.

• *Develop Web sites where visitors can find information about your products. Aim:* More bang for the buck because you're marketing only to prospects, not wasting money on other consumers.

Another new and inexpensive way to reach consumers who give their consent is by "opt-in" E-mail. You send E-mail with useful information to a general customer list. In the E-mail, give recipients an option to reply if they want to receive future E-mails.

• *Targeted word of mouth.* When possible, find out which other local businesses your customers patronize. This type of information can pay off big in word-of-mouth marketing campaigns.

EXAMPLE: When a restaurant recently discovered that many of its clients also patronized local hair salons, it gave two free meals to the owners of every salon in the area. The salon owners later told their customers about the great meals they had. Today, the restaurant is so popular that diners often have to wait for tables. And the restaurant's marketing cost was minuscule.

• *Marketing through clubs.* Many community organizations—such as church groups, civic clubs and chambers of commerce—invite business owners to speak on topics that interest their members. Take advantage of these free opportunities to cultivate new customers.

Members of a law firm can talk about wills...owners of an ad agency can speak on Internet marketing... realtors can tell club members how to increase the sale value of their houses.

Many groups won't let you make a direct sales pitch in your speech, but most of them will allow speakers to hand out information about their companies afterward. In addition to public speaking, offer to write articles or columns for the local paper. Volunteer to write the columns for free, but include your name, phone number and Web site address at the end of the articles.

BONUS: Once an article is published, you can get even more mileage from it by using reprints in mailings and other promotional materials.

VALUE vs. PRICE...

When big companies use their financial strength to discount prices to move product, the temptation on the part of smaller rivals is to follow with their own price cuts.

TRAP: By cutting prices, you shave your profit, without any guarantee of keeping customers. In fact, bargain hunters are generally the worst customers for small businesses because they're inherently disloyal.

Also—recent studies show that only 16% of consumers look for the lowest prices. A huge majority cares more about value and service.

OPPORTUNITY: Keep prices stable and target customers who shop for value and who appreciate personal service. **HOW TO DO IT...**

• *Offer freebees.* Giving out free samples is a promotional tactic that has been used for a long time by companies of all sizes. Many small businesses can gain an edge over larger rivals by also offering free consultations, seminars, clinics or demonstrations.

• *Build relationships.* Get to know customers by name, and use their names when you greet them. Always make a point of taking time to chat with them when they visit your establishment. That's one of the tactics used by two small book dealers that have actually prospered since Borders and Barnes & Noble moved into their areas.

• *Respond personally.* Use the phone when responding to people who contact you on the Internet.

• *Collect customer data.* As you get to know your customers better and better, ask them about other places they shop, radio and TV stations they prefer, sports teams they like and activities their kids enjoy. About 30% of them will usually complete a short questionnaire of this type.

Then, when you do a year-end holiday mailing, for instance, write "Go Dolphins" to a good customer whose questionnaire told you he's a fan of the team...or to another customer you could write, "Congratulations on your daughter being named to the cheerleading squad."

This extra effort develops loyalty that big companies can only dream about.

• *Follow up.* Write to customers within one month after a purchase. Ask if they're happy with the product or have any questions. Don't try to sell them anything at that time. This low-cost gesture helps them trust you and lets them know you're not trying to sell them something every time you communicate with them, as many large companies do.

• *Ask for referrals.* Referrals of new prospects are vital to small businesses because they're the most cost-effective way to increase sales.

HOW TO GET THEM: Send customers a letter that explains how important referrals are to your business. Ask for no more than three names of people who would benefit from being contacted by your company. Enclose a postage-paid envelope with your request, and offer a small gift or discount on future purchases in exchange for their response.

A large percentage of the recipients will be eager to supply names, especially if you've treated them as a valued customer.

CAUTION: Don't undermine the power of the personal touch by misusing state-of-the-art phone systems that can give small companies the image of giant corporations. The phone system won't fool new customers for long. And existing customers, who know you work out of the den in your house, for example, may resent being put on hold while they're switched to the "product development department."

It is always more effective to be who you are...especially when you are trying to build relationships with individual customers.

• *Local bulletin boards.* You won't learn about them in business schools, but community bulletin boards are a virtually free way to get your marketing message to a highly targeted audience. You can find them at grocery stores, college campuses, community centers, etc.

Bulletin boards can be particularly effective if you select those that are placed in locations frequented by likely prospects.

EXAMPLE: Notices for used furniture companies posted on bulletin boards in areas with a high concentration of young home owners.

In San Francisco, bulletin boards have become such an effective marketing medium that at least two consulting companies now help clients select bulletin board locations for their products and services.

■

BEST WAYS TO BOOST COLLECTIONS

Source: **Carol Frischer**, collections consultant, Parks Palmer Business Services, Inc., CPA business management firm, Los Angeles, and author of *Collections Made Easy: Fast, Efficient, Proven Techniques to Get Cash from Your Customers.* Career Press.

When making business-to-business collection calls, you can expect debtors to have well-prepared excuses...you aren't the only one calling them. To get past excuses and get paid, be prepared for every excuse you might hear.

EFFECTIVE: Be polite and assume that the excuse the debtor gives is valid. Don't threaten. Instead, take constructive steps to remove the excuse. **EXAMPLES...**

• *We never received a bill.* Immediately send another bill by fax, E-mail or certified mail. Get a promise of prompt payment when the bill is received.

• *The check is in the mail.* Ask when it was sent and verify that it was sent to the correct address. After 10 days, if the check hasn't arrived, ask the debtor to stop payment on it and send another by Express Mail with you paying the express charge.

• *The computer prints checks at the end of the month.* Ask when checks are printed and when they must be submitted to be paid in each cycle. Time future invoices accordingly. Call during each cycle to assure that you are being paid.

• *The computer is down. Ask a series of questions such as:* Why can't you write a check manually?...When will the computer be up?...What's being done to fix it?...How can you operate without it for so long?...How are other tasks accomplished without it? The debtor will have to make so many excuses that often writing a check will be the easier option.

• *We're expecting a big check soon and will be able to pay you in full.* Say you'll be happy to accept partial payment now, and they'll be better off by reducing late charges and protecting their credit record.

■